IMMIGRATION IN THE 21ST CENTURY:
POLITICAL, SOCIAL AND ECONOMIC ISSUES

BARRIERS AND MIGRATION CONTROL ALONG U.S. BORDERS

BACKGROUND, ISSUES AND STATUTORY AUTHORITY

IMMIGRATION IN THE 21ST CENTURY: POLITICAL, SOCIAL AND ECONOMIC ISSUES

Additional books in this series can be found on Nova's website under the Series tab.

Additional e-books in this series can be found on Nova's website under the e-book tab.

IMMIGRATION IN THE 21ST CENTURY:
POLITICAL, SOCIAL AND ECONOMIC ISSUES

BARRIERS AND MIGRATION CONTROL ALONG U.S. BORDERS

BACKGROUND, ISSUES AND STATUTORY AUTHORITY

EDITOR NAME
EDITOR

nova publishers
New York

Library of Congress Cataloging-in-Publication Data

ISBN: 978-1-63483-308-0

Published by Nova Science Publishers, Inc. † New York

CONTENTS

Preface		**vii**
Chapter 1	Border Security: Immigration Enforcement Between Ports of Entry *Lisa Seghetti*	**1**
Chapter 2	Barriers Along the U.S. Borders: Key Authorities and Requirements *Michael John Garcia*	**61**
Index		**115**

PREFACE

Border enforcement is a core element of the Department of Homeland Security's effort to control unauthorized migration, with the U.S. Border Patrol (USBP) within the U.S. Customs and Border Protection (CBP) as the lead agency along most of the border. Border enforcement has been an ongoing subject of congressional interest since the 1970s, when illegal immigration to the United States first registered as a serious national problem; and border security has received additional attention in the years since the terrorist attacks of 2001. This book reviews efforts to combat unauthorized migration across the Southwest border in the nearly three decades since IRCA initiated the modern era in migration control. In reviewing such efforts, the book takes stock of the current state of border security and considers lessons that may be learned about enhanced enforcement at U.S. borders. Furthermore, the title discusses key statutory authorities and requirements governing DHS's construction of barriers along the U.S. borders. It also includes appendixes listing federal laws that have been waived by DHS in furtherance of border construction projects.

In: Barriers and Migration Control
Editor: Arthur Rivera

ISBN: 978-1-63483-308-0

Chapter 1

BORDER SECURITY: IMMIGRATION ENFORCEMENT BETWEEN PORTS OF ENTRY*

Lisa Seghetti

SUMMARY

Border enforcement is a core element of the Department of Homeland Security's effort to control unauthorized migration, with the U.S. Border Patrol (USBP) within the U.S. Customs and Border Protection (CBP) as the lead agency along most of the border. Border enforcement has been an ongoing subject of congressional interest since the 1970s, when illegal immigration to the United States first registered as a serious national problem; and border security has received additional attention in the years since the terrorist attacks of 2001.

Since the 1990s, migration control at the border has been guided by a strategy of "prevention through deterrence"—the idea that the concentration of personnel, infrastructure, and surveillance technology along heavily trafficked regions of the border will discourage unauthorized aliens from attempting to enter the United States. Since 2005, CBP has attempted to discourage repeat illegal migrant entries and disrupt migrant smuggling networks by imposing tougher penalties

* This is an edited, reformatted and augmented version of a Congressional Research Service publication R42138, prepared for Members and Committees of Congress, dated December 31, 2014.

against certain unauthorized aliens, a set of policies eventually described as "enforcement with consequences." Most people apprehended at the Southwest border are now subject to "high consequence" enforcement outcomes.

Across a variety of indicators, the United States has substantially expanded border enforcement resources over the last three decades. Particularly since 2001, such increases include border security appropriations, personnel, fencing and infrastructure, and surveillance technology. In addition to increased resources, the USBP has implemented several strategies over the past several decades in an attempt to thwart illegal migration. Recently, the Obama Administration announced executive actions to "fix" the immigration system. These actions address numerous issues, including a revised security plan at the southern border.

The Border Patrol collects data on several different border enforcement outcomes; and this report describes trends in border apprehensions, recidivism, and estimated got aways and turn backs. Yet none of these existing data are designed to measure illegal border flows or the degree to which the border is secured. Thus, the report also describes methods for estimating illegal border flows based on enforcement data and migrant surveys.

Drawing on multiple data sources, the report suggests conclusions about the state of border security. Robust investments at the border were not associated with reduced illegal inflows during the 1980s and 1990s, but a range of evidence suggests a substantial drop in illegal inflows in 2007-2011, followed by a slight rise in 2012 and a more dramatic rise in 2013. Enforcement, along with the economic downturn in the United States, likely contributed to the drop in unauthorized migration, though the precise share of the decline attributable to enforcement is unknown.

Enhanced border enforcement also may have contributed to a number of secondary costs and benefits. To the extent that border enforcement successfully deters illegal entries, such enforcement may reduce border-area violence and migrant deaths, protect fragile border ecosystems, and improve the quality of life in border communities. But to the extent that aliens are not deterred, the concentration of enforcement resources on the border may increase border area violence and migrant deaths, encourage unauthorized migrants to find new ways to enter illegally and to remain in the United States for longer periods of time, damage border ecosystems, harm border-area businesses and the quality of life in border communities, and strain U.S. relations with Mexico and Canada.

INTRODUCTION

The country's immigration and naturalization laws have been subjects of episodic controversy since America's founding, but *illegal* immigration only became an issue in the early 20th century, when Congress passed the first strict restrictions on legal admissions. Illegal immigration declined during the Great Depression and during and after World War II, when most labor migration occurred through the U.S.-Mexico Bracero program.[1] Immigration control re-emerged as a national concern during the 1970s, when the end of the Bracero program, new restrictions on Western Hemisphere migration, and growing U.S. demand for foreign-born workers combined to cause a sharp increase in unauthorized migration flows.[2]

Congress responded in 1986 by passing the Immigration Reform and Control Act (IRCA, P.L. 99- 603), which authorized a 50% increase in Border Patrol staffing, among other provisions. Border security[3] has remained a persistent topic of congressional interest since then, and enforcement programs and appropriations have grown accordingly, as described in this report.

Despite a growing enforcement response, however, illegal immigration continued to increase over most of the next three decades.[4] Unauthorized migration declined after 2007; however, in 2013 the number of unauthorized migrants increased to 13.1 million.[5] Apprehensions of unauthorized migrants at the U.S.-Mexico border fell from about 1.2 million in FY2005 to a 41-year low of 328,000 in 2011, before climbing to 357,000 in FY2012. Apprehensions of unauthorized migrants at the U.S.-Mexico border increased to 479,377 in FY2014.[6]

Recently, the Obama Administration announced executive actions to "fix" the immigration system.[7] These actions address numerous issues, including a security plan at the southern border. Some Members of Congress and state officials, however, disagree with the President's plan and have called on the Administration to do more to secure the border.[8] Border security has been a recurrent theme in Congress's debate about immigration reform since 2005, and some Members of Congress have argued that Congress should not consider additional immigration reforms until the border is more secure.[9]

This report reviews efforts to combat unauthorized migration across the Southwest border in the nearly three decades since IRCA initiated the modern era in migration control. In reviewing such efforts, the report takes stock of the current state of border security and considers lessons that may be learned about enhanced enforcement at U.S. borders. The report begins by reviewing the history of border control and the development of a national border control strategy beginning in the 1990s. The following sections summarize appropriations and resources dedicated to border enforcement, indicators of enforcement outcomes, metrics for estimating unauthorized migration flows, and possible secondary and unintended consequences of border enforcement. The report concludes by reviewing the overall costs and benefits of the current approach to migration control and raising additional questions that may help guide the discussion of these issues in the future.

BORDER PATROL HISTORY AND STRATEGY

Congress created the U.S. Border Patrol (USBP) within the Department of Commerce and Labor by an appropriations act in 1924,[10] two days after passing the first permanent numeric immigration restrictions.[11] Numerical limits only applied to the Eastern Hemisphere, barring most Asian immigration; and the Border Patrol's initial focus was on preventing the entry of Chinese migrants, as well as combating gun trafficking and alcohol imports during prohibition. The majority of agents were stationed on the northern border.[12] The Border Patrol became part of the new Immigration and Naturalization Service (INS) in 1933, and the INS moved from the Department of Labor to the Department of Justice in 1940. The Border Patrol's focus shifted to the Southwest border during World War II, but preventing illegal migration across the Southwest border remained a low priority during most of the 20th century.[13]

Illegal migration from Mexico increased after 1965 as legislative changes restricted legal Mexican immigration at the same time that social and economic changes caused stronger migration "pushes" in Mexico (e.g., inadequate employment opportunities) and stronger "pulls" in the United States (e.g., employment opportunities, links to migrant communities in Mexico).[14] Congress held hearings on illegal immigration beginning in 1971, and after more than a decade of debate passed the Immigration Reform and Control Act of 1986 (IRCA, P.L. 99-603), which described border enforcement as an "essential element" of immigration control and authorized a 50% increase in funding for the Border Patrol, among other provisions.[15] Congress passed at least 11 additional laws addressing illegal immigration over the next two decades, 7 of which included provisions related to the border.[16]

Border Patrol Strategic Plans

Seventy years after it began operations, the Border Patrol developed its first formal national border control strategy in 1994, the National Strategic Plan. The plan was updated in 2004 and again in 2012.

National Strategic Plan

The National Strategic Plan (NSP) was developed in 1994 in response to a widespread perception that the Southwest border was being overrun by unauthorized immigration and drug smuggling, and to respond to a study commissioned by the Office of National Drug Control Policy. The study recommended that the INS change its approach from arresting unauthorized immigrants after they enter the United States, as had previously been the case, to focus instead on preventing their entry.[17] Under the new approach, the INS would place personnel, surveillance technology, fencing, and other infrastructure directly on the border to discourage illegal flows, a strategy that became known as "prevention through deterrence." According to the 1994 INS plan, "the prediction is that with traditional entry and smuggling routes disrupted, illegal traffic will be deterred, or forced over more hostile terrain, less suited for crossing and more suited for enforcement."[18]

The strategy had four phases that began with the border patrol sectors with the highest levels of illegal immigration activity.

- Phase I: San Diego, CA, and El Paso, TX, sectors;
- Phase II: Tucson, AZ, Del Rio, TX, Laredo, TX, and McAllen, TX, sectors;
- Phase III: El Centro, CA, Yuma, AZ, and Marfa, TX, sectors; and
- Phase IV: The northern border, gulf coast, and coastal waterways.

The strategy yielded several initiatives aimed at stemming illegal immigration and human smuggling, and interdicting drug trafficking. These initiatives included the following:

- *Operation Gatekeeper* was first initiated at the San Diego Border Patrol Sector and was later extended to the El Centro Border Patrol Sector. The initiative involved providing border patrol agents with additional resources, such as increased staffing and new technologies.

- *Operation Safeguard* was initiated at the Tucson Border Patrol Sector and was aimed at stemming illegal immigration by pushing illegal immigrants away from urban areas.
- *Operation Hold the Line* was initiated at the El Paso Border Patrol Sector and was aimed at the specific needs of the community. New border patrol agents were added to the area and innovative resources were deployed, including IDENT[19] terminals. The initiative also included the installation of fences along parts of the border and other infrastructure improvements.
- Operation Rio Grande was initiated at the McAllen Border Patrol Sector and focused on increasing the number of border patrol agents.

The implementation of Phase II and subsequent phases was to be based on the success of Phase I, with the plan describing several expected indicators of effective border enforcement, including an initial increase of border arrests and entry attempt to be followed by an eventual reduction of arrests, a change in traditional traffic patterns, and an increase in more sophisticated smuggling methods.[20] As predicted, apprehensions within the San Diego and El Paso sectors fell sharply beginning in 1994-1995, and traffic patterns shifted, primarily to the Tucson and South Texas (Rio Grande Valley) sectors (see "Southwest Border Apprehensions by Sector"). A 1997 General Accounting Office (GAO) report was cautiously optimistic about the strategy.[21]

Congress supported the prevention through deterrence approach. In 1996, House and Senate appropriators directed the INS to hire new agents and to reallocate personnel from the interior to front line duty.[22] And the Illegal Immigration Reform and Immigrant Responsibility Act of 1996 (P.L. 104-208) expressly authorized the construction and improvement of fencing and other barriers along the Southwest border and required the completion of a triple-layered fence along 14 miles of the border near San Diego where the INS had begun to install fencing in 1990.[23]

National Border Patrol Strategy

In the wake of the September 11, 2001, terrorist attacks, the USBP refocused its priorities on preventing terrorist penetration, while remaining committed to its traditional duties of preventing the illicit trafficking of people and contraband between official ports of entry. Shortly after the creation of DHS, the USBP was directed to formulate a new National Border Patrol Strategy (NBPS) that would better reflect the realities of the post-9/11 security landscape. In March 2004, the Border Patrol unveiled the National Border

Patrol Strategy, which placed greater emphasis on interdicting terrorists and featured five main objectives:

- establishing the substantial probability of apprehending terrorists and their weapons as they attempt to enter illegally between the ports of entry;
- deterring illegal entries through improved enforcement;
- detecting, apprehending, and deterring smugglers of humans, drugs, and other contraband;
- leveraging "Smart Border" technology to multiply the deterrent and enforcement effect of agents; and
- reducing crime in border communities, thereby improving the quality of life and economic vitality of those areas.[24]

The NBPS was an attempt to lay the foundation for achieving "operational control" over the border, defined by the Border Patrol as "the ability to detect, respond, and interdict border penetrations in areas deemed as high priority for threat potential or other national security objectives."[25] The strategy emphasized a hierarchical and vertical command structure, featuring a direct chain of command from headquarters to the field. The document emphasized the use of tactical, operational, and strategic intelligence and sophisticated surveillance systems to assess risk and target enforcement efforts; and the rapid deployment of USBP agents to respond to emerging threats. Additionally, the plan called for the Border Patrol to coordinate closely with CBP's Office of Intelligence and other federal intelligence agencies.

Border Patrol Strategic Plan

CBP published a new Border Patrol Strategic Plan (BPSP) in May 2012 that shifted attention from resource acquisition and deployment to the strategic allocation of resources by "focusing enhanced capabilities against the highest threats and rapidly responding along the border."[26] From an operational perspective, the 2012 plan emphasizes the collection and analysis of information about evolving border threats; integration of Border Patrol and CBP planning across different border sectors and among the full range of federal, state, local, tribal, and international organizations involved in border security operations; and rapid Border Patrol response to specific border threats.[27]

DHS Secure Border Initiative

The Border Patrol's approach to border enforcement has been mirrored in broader DHS policies. In November 2005, the Department of Homeland Security announced a comprehensive multiyear plan, the Secure Border Initiative (SBI), to secure U.S. borders and reduce illegal migration.[28] Under SBI, DHS announced plans to obtain operational control of the northern and southern borders within five years by focusing attention in five main areas:

- *Increased staffing.* As part of SBI, DHS announced the addition of 1,000 new Border Patrol agents, 250 new ICE investigators targeting human smuggling operations, and 500 other new ICE agents and officers.[29]
- *Improved detention and removal capacity.* Historically, most non-Mexicans apprehended at the border were placed in formal removal proceedings.[30] Yet backlogs in the immigration court system meant that most such aliens were released on bail or on their own recognizance prior to a removal hearing, and many failed to show up for their hearings.[31] In October 2005, DHS announced plans to detain 100% of non-Mexicans apprehended at the border until they could be processed for removal. SBI supported this goal by adding detention capacity, initially increasing bed space by 2,000 to a total of 20,000.[32] On August 23, 2006, DHS announced that the policy to "end catch and release" had been successfully implemented.[33]
- *Surveillance technology.* SBI included plans to expand DHS's use of surveillance technology between ports of entry, including unmanned aerial vehicle (UAV) systems, other aerial assets, remote video surveillance (RVS) systems, and ground sensors.[34] These tools were to be linked into a common integrated system that became known as SBI*net* (see "Surveillance Assets" below).
- *Tactical infrastructure.* SBI continued DHS's commitment to the expansion of border fencing, roads, and stadium-style lighting.[35]
- ***Interior enforcement.*** SBI also included plans to expand enforcement within the United States at worksites and through state and local partnerships, jail screening programs, and task forces to locate fugitive aliens.[36]

CBP Consequence Delivery System

Although not the subject of a formal public policy document like those discussed above, an additional component of CBP's approach to border control in recent years has been an effort to promote "high consequence" enforcement for unauthorized Mexicans apprehended at the border. Historically, immigration agents permitted most Mexicans apprehended at the border to voluntarily return to Mexico without any penalty.[37] Since 2005, CBP has limited voluntary returns in favor of three types of "high consequence" outcomes:

- *Formal Removal.*[38] Aliens[39] formally removed from the United States generally are ineligible for a visa (i.e., inadmissible) for at least five years,[40] and they may be subject to criminal charges if they illegally reenter the United States.[41] Prior to 2005, most unauthorized Mexicans apprehended at the border were not placed in removal proceedings, in part because standard removal procedures require an appearance before an immigration judge and are resource intensive.[42] Since 2005, CBP has relied extensively on two provisions in the Immigration and Nationality Act (INA) that permit aliens to be formally removed with limited judicial processing. Under INA Section 235(b), certain arriving aliens are subject to "expedited removal" (ER) without additional hearing or review.[43] ER was added to the INA in 1996, but initially was reserved for aliens apprehended at ports of entry. In a series of four announcements between November 2002 and January 2006, DHS expanded the use of ER to include certain aliens who had entered the United States within the previous two weeks and who were apprehended anywhere within 100 miles of a U.S. land or coastal border.[44] Under INA Section 241(a)(5), an alien who reenters the United States after being formally removed or departing under a removal order is subject to "reinstatement of removal" without reopening or reviewing the original removal order.[45]
- *Criminal Charges.* Unauthorized aliens apprehended at the border may face federal immigration charges,[46] but historically, most such aliens have not been charged with a crime. Working with the Department of Justice (DOJ), DHS has increased the proportion of people apprehended at the border who are charged with immigration-related criminal offenses. A portion of aliens facing criminal charges in Southwest border districts are prosecuted through the "Operation

Streamline" program (see accompanying text box). Mexicans apprehended in the United States who are found to be smuggling aliens may also be subject to criminal charges in Mexico under the U.S.-Mexican Operation Against Smugglers Initiative on Safety and Security (OASISS).[47]

- *Remote repatriation.* CBP uses a pair of programs to return Mexicans to remote locations rather than to the nearest Mexican port of entry. Under the Alien Transfer Exit Program (ATEP), certain Mexicans apprehended near the border are repatriated to border ports hundreds of miles away—typically moving people from Arizona to Texas or California—a process commonly described as "lateral repatriation."[48] Under the Mexican Interior Repatriation Program (MIRP), certain Mexican nationals are repatriated to their home towns within Mexico rather than being returned just across the border.[49]

In general, these high consequence enforcement outcomes are intended to deter illegal flows by raising the costs to migrants of being apprehended and by making it more difficult for them to reconnect with smugglers following a failed entry attempt.[50] To manage these disparate programs, CBP has designed the "Consequence Delivery System.... to uniquely evaluate each subject [who is apprehended] and identify the ideal consequences to deliver to impede and deter further illegal activity."[51] USBP agents use laminated cards with matrices describing the range of enforcement actions available for a particular alien as a function of the person's immigration and criminal histories, among other factors, and of the enforcement resources available in each Border Patrol sector. According to public comments by then CBP Commissioner Alan Bersin, the goal of the Consequence Delivery System, in certain sectors of the border, is to ensure that virtually everyone who is apprehended faces "some type of consequence" other than voluntary return.[52]

As *Figure 1* indicates, the effort to limit voluntary returns in favor of "high consequence" enforcement outcomes has, to a great degree, been implemented. The figure depicts Southwest border apprehensions (the solid line) and the four main types of enforcement outcomes (voluntary returns, criminal charges, formal removal, and remote repatriation—the shaded areas) for FY2005-FY2012.[53] (Enforcement outcomes exceed apprehensions because some aliens face more than one outcome, such as formal removal along with lateral repatriation. In addition, certain aliens apprehended in one fiscal year do not complete their case processing until the following year)

Operation Streamline

Operation Streamline is a partnership program among CBP, U.S. Attorneys, and District Court judges in certain border districts to expedite criminal justice processing. The program permits groups of criminal defendants to have their cases heard at the same time, rather than requiring judges to review individual charges, and arranges in most cases for aliens facing felony charges for illegal re-entry to plead guilty to misdemeanor illegal entry charges—a plea bargain that leads to the rapid resolution of cases. Although Operation Streamline has been described as a zero tolerance program leading to prosecutions for 100% of apprehended aliens, the program confronts limits in judicial and detention capacity, resulting in daily caps on the number of people facing charges in certain districts. In the Tucson sector, for example, the courts reportedly limit Streamline cases to about 70 prosecutions per day.

Operation Streamline was established in the USBP's Del Rio Sector in December 2005 and expanded to the Yuma Sector in December 2006, Laredo Sector in October 2007, Tucson Sector in January 2008, and Rio Grande Valley Sector in June 2008. The program mainly consists of procedural arrangements among DHS and DOJ officials at the local level, and 15 CBP agents have been detailed to DOJ in three Border Patrol sectors to assist DOJ attorneys and U.S. Marshalls with prosecutions. A total of 208,939 people were processed through Operation Streamline through the end of FY2012—about 45% of the 463,051 immigration-related prosecutions in Southwest border districts during this period.

On October 17, 2014, House Judiciary Committee Chairman Goodlatte issued a press release that included the text of a letter he sent to Attorney General Eric Holder. In the letter, Chairman Goodlatte expressed concern over the decrease in the number of prosecutions under Operation Streamline for first-time illegal border crossers. According to the Yuma County (AZ) Sheriff, the U.S. Attorney's Office for the District of Arizona will cease prosecuting first-time illegal border crossers, and only undocumented aliens with an adverse immigration history (not including aliens who were processed under voluntary return and voluntary departure) will be prosecuted under immigration law.

Sources: CBP Office of Congressional Affairs; National Research Council Committee on Estimating Costs of Immigration Enforcement in the Department of Justice, Budgeting for Immigration Enforcement: A Path to Better

Performance (Washington, DC: National Academies Press, 2011); House Judiciary Committee, Chairman Bob Goodlatte, "Goodlatte Seeks Answers About the Drop in the Number of Prosecutions for First-Time Illegal Border Crossers," press release, Oct. 17, 2014; and Yuma County Sheriff's Office, letter to Senator Jeff Flake, Aug. 19, 2014.

As the figure illustrates, voluntary return fell from 77% of all enforcement outcomes in 2005 (956,470 out of 1,238,554) to 14% in FY2012 (76,664 out of 529,393). Conversely, the proportion of enforcement outcomes that were high consequence outcomes (i.e., criminal charges, formal removal, or remote repatriation) increased from 23% (282,084 out of 1,238,554) in FY2005 to 86% in FY2012 (452,664 out of 529,393).

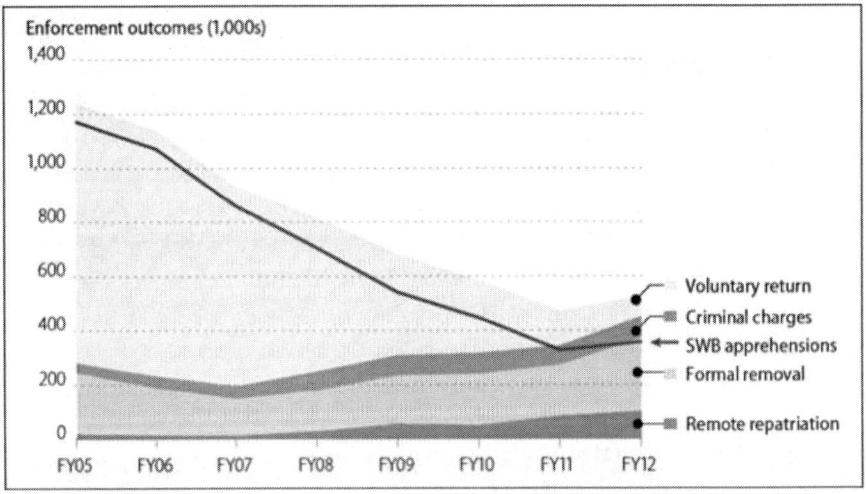

Sources: CRS presentation of data provided by CBP Office of Congressional Affairs March 10, 2013; ICE Office of Congressional Affairs March 22, 2013; Administrative Office of the U.S. Courts. CRS attempted to obtain more current data (i.e., FY2013 and FY2014); however, according to DHS the data are not available for release (CRS email with DHS Congressional Affairs office on November 13, 2014).

Notes: Immigration-related criminal charges may include some U.S. citizens and lawful aliens.

Figure 1. CBP "Enforcement with Consequences," FY2005-FY2012 (Southwest Border).

One factor that has facilitated the rise in the proportion of apprehensions subject to high-consequence enforcement has been a sharp drop in the number of aliens apprehended on the Southwest border, as discussed in this report (see "Alien Apprehensions"). Nonetheless, as *Figure 1* also illustrates, CBP's effort to expand high-consequence enforcement has resulted in a rise in removals, prosecutions, and lateral/interior repatriations since 2007, even during a period of falling border apprehensions.

With the implementation of the Consequence Delivery System, the Border Patrol has initiated a system to estimate the deterrent effect of different enforcement outcomes. In particular, the Border Patrol tracks, for each of 10 different enforcement consequences, the percentage of aliens who were re-apprehended during the same fiscal year following repatriation (i.e., the recidivism rate). These recidivism rates are reported in *Table 1*.[54]

As *Table 1* indicates, several consequences were associated with recidivism rates well *below* the overall FY2012 average of 16.7%. These low recidivism consequences included standard removal proceedings following a notice to appear (3.8%), standard criminal prosecutions (9.1%), criminal charges through the OASISS program (10.2%), and Operation Streamline (10.3%). Recidivism rates were also lower than the FY2011 average of 19.8% for aliens returned to Mexico through the MIRP program (9.3%) in that year. (MIRP did not operate in FY2012). Conversely, recidivism rates in FY2012 were well *above* the overall average for aliens subject to voluntary return (27.1%) and for aliens subject to lateral repatriation through the ATEP program (23.8%).[55]

The differences in recidivism rates may not be wholly attributable to differences among the consequences because the Border Patrol takes account of aliens' migration histories and other factors when assigning people to different enforcement outcomes. Nonetheless, these data suggest that standard removal and criminal charges have a stronger deterrent effect on future unauthorized migration than does voluntary return. Conversely, lateral repatriation appears to do little to discourage people from reentering the United States.[56]

Southern Border Campaign Plan[57]

In a November 20, 2014, memo, Secretary Johnson "commissions" three Joint Task Forces.[58] According to Secretary Johnson, the three Joint Task Forces will bring together personnel from CBP as well as other DHS agencies—U.S. Coast Guard (USCG), U.S. Immigration and Customs Enforcement (ICE), and U.S. Citizenship and Immigration Services (USCIS).

Table 1. Consequence Delivery System Outcomes and Recidivism Rates (Southwest Border)

Consequence		FY2011 Number of Cases	Recidivism Rate	FY2012 Number of Cases	Recidivism Rate
Criminal Charges	OASISS	533	14.7%	429	10.2%
	Operation Streamline	36,871	12.1%	44,300	10.3%
	Standard Prosecution	31,130	9.1%	34,839	9.1%
Formal Removal	Notice to Appear	20,923	6.6%	23,491	3.8%
	Expedited Removal	39,855	16.6%	148,548	16.4%
	Reinstatement	74,106	16.9%	98,424	15.9%
	Quick Court	2,730	19.0%	1,070	18.3%
Remote Repatriation	MIRP	8,940	9.3%	0	NA[a]
	ATEP	75,966	27.8%	101,992	23.8%
Voluntary Return		129,207	29.4%	76,664	27.1%
Total Cases		318,883	19.8%	347,921	16.7%

Source: CRS analysis based on data provided by CBP Office of Congressional Affairs, March 10, 2013.

Notes: OASISS stands for the U.S.-Mexican Operation Against Smugglers Initiative on Safety and Security. See text for discussions of Operation Streamline, expedited removal, and reinstatement of removal. Standard Prosecution refers to criminal charges through the standard federal prosecution process. Notice to appear is the first stage in the standard formal removal process before an immigration judge. Quick court is a program involving expedited removal hearings before an immigration judge. MIRP stands for the Mexico Interior Repatriation Program. ATEP stands for the Alien Transfer Exchange Program. Total Cases refers to the total number of apprehensions and border-wide overall recidivism rate. The sum of the consequences exceeds the number of total cases because some people are subject to more than one consequence.

[a] MIRP did not operate in FY2012.

The Joint Task Forces will also "integrate capabilities of the remaining [DHS] components as needed."[59] According to Secretary Johnson, "Two of these task forces will be geographically based and one will be functionally focused."[60] Joint Task Force East will cover "the Southern maritime border and approaches."[61] Joint Task Force West will have responsibility for the southern land border and the West Coast, while an entity dubbed Joint Task Force Investigations "will focus on investigations in support of the geographic Task Forces."[62] The memo lays out broad missions and objectives and sets a 90-day timeframe to "realign personnel and stand up headquarters capabilities within each Joint Task Force."[63]

BUDGET AND RESOURCES

Statutory and strategic changes since 1986 are reflected in border enforcement appropriations and in CBP's assets at the border, including personnel, infrastructure, and surveillance technology. This section reviews trends in each of these areas.

Border Security Appropriations

Figure 2 depicts U.S. Border Patrol appropriations for FY1989-FY2013. Appropriations have grown steadily over this period, rising from $232 million in 1989 to $1.3 billion in FY2002 (the last data available prior to the creation of DHS), $3.8 billion in FY2010, and $3.7 billion in FY2014.[64] The largest growth came following the formation of DHS in FY2003, reflecting Congress's focus on border security in the aftermath of 9/11.

Appropriations reported in *Figure 2* are only a *subset* of all border security funding. These data do not include, for example, additional CBP sub-accounts funding Headquarters Management and Administration ($1.2 billion in FY2014), and Border Security Inspections and Trade Facilitation at Ports of Entry ($3.2 billion in FY2014); or additional CBP accounts funding Border Security Fencing, Infrastructure, and Technology ($351 million in FY2014); Air and Marine Operations ($805 million in FY2014) and Facilities Management ($456 million in FY2014).[65] A substantial portion of these accounts is dedicated to border security and immigration enforcement, as these terms are commonly used. The data in *Figure 2* also exclude U.S. Immigration and Customs Enforcement (ICE) appropriations, which totaled $5.2 billion for Salaries and Expenses for FY2014.[66] About a quarter of ICE's 20,000 personnel reportedly are deployed to the Southwest border.[67]

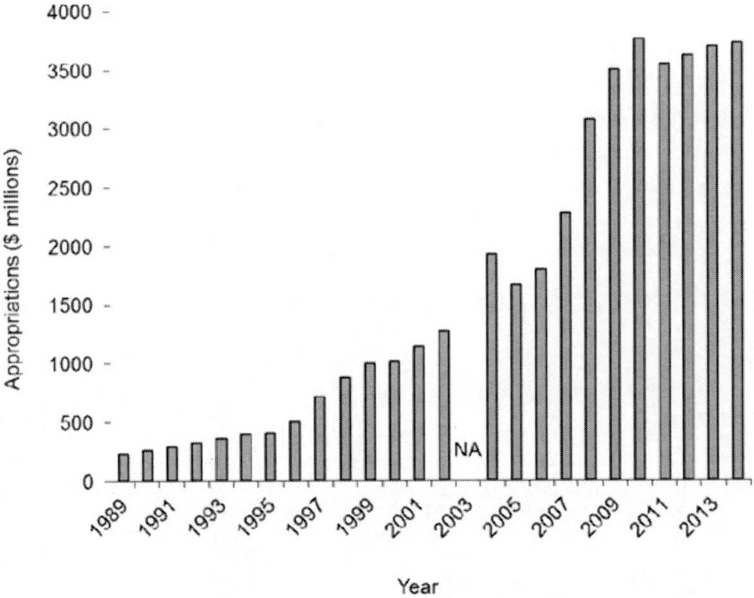

Sources: INS Congressional Budget Justification FY1991-FY2002; DHS Appropriations reports FY2004-FY2014.

Notes: Appropriations for 1989-2002 reflect the "Border Patrol" sub-account of the INS Salaries and Expenses account of the DOJ annual appropriations. Appropriations for 2004-2014 reflect the "Border Security and Control between Ports of Entry" sub-account of the CBP Salaries and Expenses account of the DHS annual appropriations. Data are not available for FY2003 because neither the INS nor congressional appropriators provided a breakout of the salaries and expenses sub-accounts within the Enforcement and Border Affairs account during that year's funding cycle. The overall Enforcement and Border Affairs account within INS for FY2003 was $2,881 million, up from $2,541 million in FY2001 and $2,740 million in FY2002. With the establishment of DHS, the former INS, customs inspections from the former U.S. Customs Service, and the U.S. Border Patrol were merged to form the Bureau of Customs and Border Protection within DHS. As a result, data for years prior to FY2003 may not be strictly comparable with data for FY2004 and after. FY2005 figure includes a $124 million supplemental appropriation from P.L. 109-13. FY2006 figure does not include any portion of the $423 million in supplemental funding for CBP Salaries and Expenses in P.L. 109-234 because the law did not specify how much of this funding was for USBP; DHS reported in its FY2008 DHS Budget Justification that the Border Patrol received a $1,900 million appropriation in FY2006. FY2010 figure includes a $176 million supplemental appropriation from P.L. 111-230. FY2013 figure includes the pre-sequester amount.

Figure 2. U.S. Border Patrol Appropriations, FY1989-FY2014.

And *Figure 2* excludes border enforcement appropriations for other federal agencies— including the Departments of Justice, Defense, the Interior, and Agriculture, all of which play a role in border security—as well as funding for the U.S. federal court system.[68]

Border Patrol Personnel

Accompanying this budget increase, Congress has passed at least four laws since 1986 authorizing increased Border Patrol personnel.[69] USBP staffing roughly doubled in the decade after the 1986 IRCA, doubled again between 1996 and the 9/11 attacks, and doubled again in the decade after 9/11 (see *Figure 3*). As of September 20, 2014, the USBP had 20,863 agents, including 18,156 posted at the Southwest border.[70]

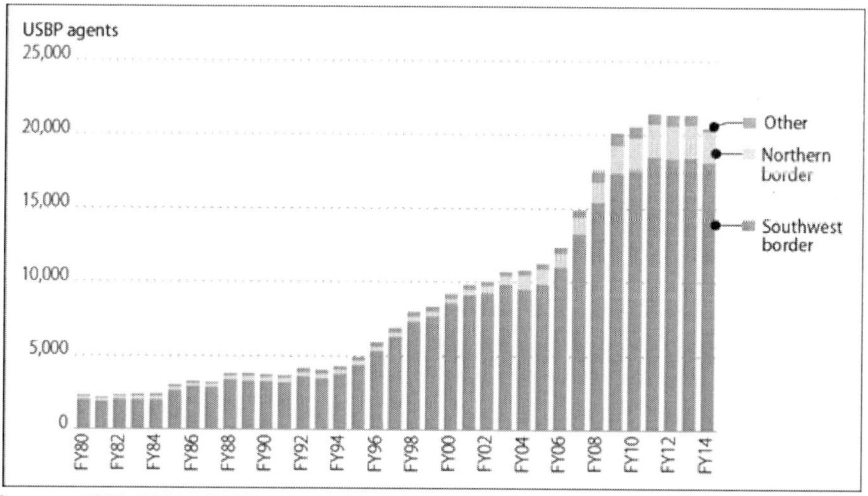

Source: 1980-1991: CRS presentation of data from Syracuse University Transactional Records Access Clearinghouse; 1992-2013: CRS presentation of data provided by CBP Office of Congressional Affairs; 2014: U.S. Customs and Border Protection, Stats and Summaries, Border Patrol Agent Staffing by Fiscal Year, http://www.cbp.gov/sites/default/files/documents/BP%20Staffing%20FY1992-FY2014_0.pdf.

Note: The total number of Border Patrol agents includes agents stationed in coastal sectors and at USBP headquarters.

Figure 3. U.S. Border Patrol Agents, Total and by Region, FY1980-FY2014.

National Guard Troops at the Border

The National Guard also is authorized to support federal, state, and local law enforcement agencies (LEAs) at the border. Basic authority for the Department of Defense (DOD, including the National Guard) to assist LEAs is contained in Chapter 18 of Title 10 of the U.S. Code, and DOD personnel are expressly authorized to maintain and operate equipment in cooperation with federal LEAs in conjunction with the enforcement of counterterrorism operations or the enforcement of counterdrug laws, immigration laws, and customs requirements.[71] DOD may assist any federal, state, or local LEA requesting counterdrug assistance under the National Defense Authorization Act, as amended.[72] Under Title 32 of the U.S. Code, National Guard personnel also may serve a federal purpose, such as border security, and receive federal pay while remaining under the command control of their respective state governors.[73]

National Guard troops were first deployed to the border on a pilot basis in 1988, when about 100 soldiers assisted the U.S. Customs Service at several Southwest border locations, and National Guard and active military units provided targeted support for the USBP's surveillance programs throughout the following decade. The first large-scale deployment of the National Guard to the border occurred in 2006-2008, when over 30,000 troops provided engineering, aviation, identification, technical, logistical, and administrative support to CBP as part of "Operation Jump Start."[74] President Obama announced an additional deployment of up to 1,200 National Guard troops to the Southwest border on May 25, 2010, with the National Guard supporting the Border Patrol, by providing intelligence work and drug and human trafficking interdiction.[75] The 2010 deployment was originally scheduled to end in June 2011, but the full deployment was extended twice (in June and September 2011). The Administration announced in December 2011 that the deployment would be reduced to fewer than 300 troops beginning in January 2012, with National Guard efforts focused on supporting DHS's aerial surveillance operations.[76] In December 2012, DHS and the Department of Defense announced that the National Guard deployment would be extended through December 2013.[77]

Fencing and Tactical Infrastructure

Border tactical infrastructure includes roads, lighting, pedestrian fencing, and vehicle barriers. Tactical infrastructure is intended to impede illicit cross-border activity, disrupt and restrict smuggling operations, and establish a substantial probability of apprehending terrorists seeking entry into the United States.[78] The former INS installed the first fencing along the U.S.-Mexican border beginning in 1990 east of the Pacific Ocean near San Diego.

Congress expressly authorized the construction and improvement of fencing and other barriers under Section 102(a) of the Illegal Immigration Reform and Immigrant Responsibility Act of 1996 (IIRIRA),[79] which also required the completion of a triple-layered fence along the original 14 mile border segment near San Diego. The Secure Fence Act of 2006[80] amended IIRIRA with a requirement for double-layered fencing along five segments of the Southwest border, totaling about 850 miles.[81] IIRIRA was amended again by the Consolidated Appropriations Act, FY2008. Under that amendment, the law now requires the Secretary of Homeland Security to construct reinforced fencing "along not less than 700 miles of the southwest border where fencing would be most practical and effective and provide for the installation of additional physical barriers, roads, lighting, cameras, and sensors to gain operational control of the southwest border."[82] The act further specifies, however, that the Secretary of Homeland Security is *not* required to install fencing "in a particular location along the international border of the United States if the Secretary determines that the use or placement of such resources is not the most appropriate means to achieve and maintain operational control over the international border at such location."[83]

As of October 2014, DHS installed 352.7 miles of primary pedestrian fencing, 299 miles of vehicle fencing (total of 651 miles), and 36.3 miles of secondary fencing. The Border Patrol reportedly had identified a total of 653 miles of the border as appropriate for fencing and barriers (i.e., 2 additional miles).[84] *Figure 4* summarizes annual appropriations for tactical infrastructure (including surveillance technology) for FY1996-FY2014. Appropriations increased from $25 million in FY1996 to $298 million in FY2006, an 11-fold increase (8-fold when adjusting for inflation), and then jumped to $1.5 billion in FY2007 as DHS created a new Border Security Fencing, Infrastructure, and Technology (BSFIT) account and appropriated money to pay for the border fencing mandate in the Secure Fence Act of 2006. BSFIT appropriations have fallen for seven consecutive years (from FY2007 through FY2013); however, in FY2014 BSFIT appropriations increased to $351 million (from $324 million from the previous fiscal year).

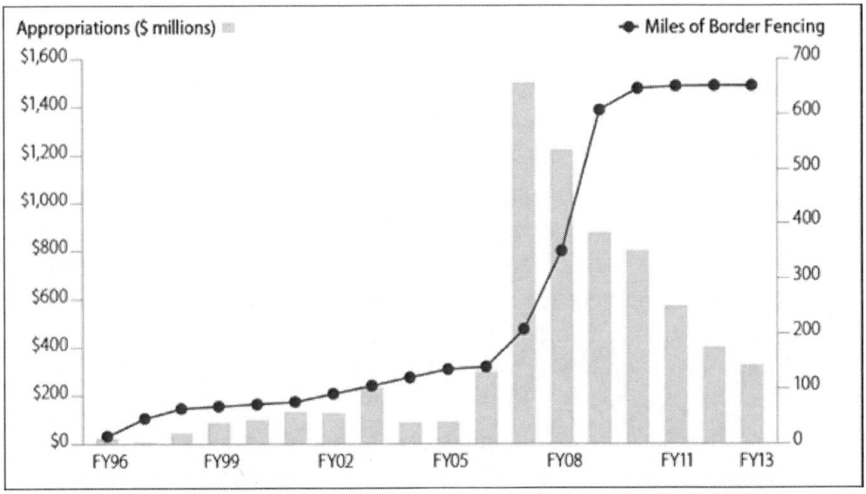

Sources: INS Congressional Budget Justifications FY2001-FY2003; DHS Congressional Budget Justifications FY2005-2007; DHS Appropriations bills FY2007-FY2013.

Notes: In FY2003, immigration inspections from the former INS, customs inspections from the former U.S. Customs Service, and USBP were merged to form the Bureau of Customs and Border Protection within DHS. As a result, data for years prior to FY2003 may not be comparable with the data for FY2004 and after. Data for FY1996-FY2002 include USBP construction and tactical infrastructure accounts. Construction account funding has been used to fund a number of projects at the border, including fencing, vehicle barriers, roads, and USBP stations and checkpoints. Funding for FY1998-FY2000 includes San Diego fencing as well as fencing, light, and road projects in El Centro, Tucson, El Paso, and Marfa. Data for FY2003-FY2006 include DHS construction and tactical appropriations. Data for FY2007-FY2012 include total appropriations to CBP's Border Security Fencing, Infrastructure, and Technology (BSFIT) account. This account funds the construction of fencing, other infrastructure such as roads and vehicle barriers, as well as border technologies such as cameras and sensors.

Figure 4. Tactical Infrastructure Appropriations and Miles of Border Fencing, FY1996-FY2013.

Surveillance Assets

The Border Patrol uses advanced technology to augment its agents' ability to patrol the border. USBP's border surveillance system has its origins in the former Immigration and Naturalization Service's (INS's) Integrated

Surveillance Information System (ISIS), initiated in 1998. ISIS was folded into a broader border surveillance system named the America's Shield Initiative (ASI) in 2005, and ASI was made part of DHS's Secure Border Initiative (SBI) the following year, with the surveillance program renamed SBI*net* and managed under contract by the Boeing Corporation.

Under all three of these names, the system consisted of a network of remote video surveillance (RVS) systems (including cameras and infrared systems), and sensors (including seismic, magnetic, and thermal detectors), linked into a computer network, known as the Integrated Computer Assisted Detection (ICAD) database. The system was intended to ensure seamless coverage of the border by combining the feeds from multiple cameras and sensors into one remote-controlled system linked to a central communications control room at a USBP station or sector headquarters. USBP personnel monitoring the control room screened the ICAD system to re-position RVS cameras toward the location where sensor alarms were tripped. Control room personnel then alerted field agents to the intrusion and coordinated the response.

All three of these systems struggled to meet deployment timelines and to provide USBP with the promised level of border surveillance.[85] DHS also faced criticism of ASI and SBI*net* for noncompetitive contracting practices, inadequate oversight of contractors, and cost overruns.[86] DHS Secretary Napolitano ordered a department-wide assessment of the SBI*net* technology project in January 2010 and suspended the SBI*net* contract in March 2010.[87] The review confirmed SBI*net*'s history of "continued and repeated technical problems, cost overruns, and schedule delays, raising serious questions about the system's ability to meet the needs for technology along the border."[88] DHS terminated SBI*net* in January 2011.

Under the department's Arizona Surveillance Technology Plan, the Border Patrol deploys a mix of different surveillance technologies designed to meet the specific needs of different border regions. As of November 2012, deployed assets included 337 Remote Video Surveillance Systems (RVSS) consisting of fixed daylight and infrared cameras that transmit images to a central location (up from 269 in 2006), 198 short and medium range Mobile Vehicle Surveillance Systems (MVSS) mounted on trucks and monitored in the truck's passenger compartment (up from zero in 2005) and 41 long range Mobile Surveillance Systems (MSS, up from zero in 2005), 12 hand-held agent portable medium range surveillance systems (APSS, up from zero in 2005), 15 Integrated Fixed Towers that were developed as part of the SBInet system (up from zero in 2005), and 13,406 unattended ground sensors (up from about 11,200 in 2005).[89] According to CBP officials, the department's acquisitions strategy emphasizes flexible equipment and mobile technology that permits USBP to surge surveillance capacity in a particular region, and off-theshelf technology in order to hold down costs and get resources on the ground more quickly.

Aerial and Marine Surveillance

In addition to these ground-based surveillance assets, CBP deploys manned and unmanned aircraft as well as marine vessels to conduct surveillance. Air and marine vessels patrol regions of the border that are inaccessible to other surveillance assets, with unmanned aerial systems (UAS) deployed in areas considered too high-risk for manned aircraft or personnel on the ground.[90] In FY2012, CBP's Office of Air and Marine deployed 19 types of aircraft and three classes of marine vessels, for a total of 269 aircraft and 293 marine vessels operating from over 70 locations.[91] The agency reported 81,045 flight hours (down from about 95,000 in FY2011) and 47,742 underway hours in marine vessels (down from about 133,000 in FY2011).[92] As of November 2012, CBP operated a total of 10 UAS up from zero in 2006, including 2 UAS on the Northern border, 5 on the Southwest border, and 3 in the Gulf of Mexico.[93] UAS accounted for 5,737 flight hours in FY2012, up from 4,406 hours in FY2011.[94]

With support from Department of Defense (DOD), CBP conducted an evaluation of two unmanned aerostat (tethered blimp) systems during the summer of 2012: the Persistent Ground Surveillance System (PGSS) and the Rapid Aerostat Initial Deployment (RAID). In addition, CBP evaluated PGSS and RAID towers, which support aerostat deployment as well as ground-based technologies. These two systems have been deployed by the military to conduct area surveillance. As a result of the evaluation, CBP concluded that these systems could provide useful support to CBP operations on the border; and CBP reportedly is working with DOD to identify opportunities to transfer ownership of aerostats returning from overseas to CBP.[95]

BORDER PATROL ENFORCEMENT DATA

For 90 years, the Border Patrol has recorded the number of deportable aliens apprehended in the United States;[96] and alien apprehensions remain the agency's primary indicator of immigration enforcement. The agency also collects several additional measures of immigration enforcement, including unique apprehensions, alien recidivism, and estimated turn backs and got aways. These enforcement outcomes provide insight into the state of the border, as discussed in this section, but they confront certain limitations when it comes to estimating illegal border inflows (see "Metrics of Border Security").

Alien Apprehensions

Figure 5 depicts total USBP apprehensions of deportable and removable aliens for FY1960- FY2014. Apprehensions are widely understood to be correlated with illegal flows, and the data in *Figure 5* reflect historical trends in unauthorized migration (see "Border Patrol History and Strategy"). Apprehensions were very low in the 1960s, but climbed sharply in the two decades after 1965. Apprehensions reached an all-time high of 1.7 million in 1986 and again in 2000, and an average of more than 1.2 million apprehensions per year were recorded 1983-2006, reflecting high levels of unauthorized migration throughout this period. As *Figure 5* also illustrates, apprehensions have fallen sharply since 2000, and particularly since 2006. The 340,252 apprehensions observed in 2011 were the lowest level since 1971, and the 364,768 apprehensions in 2012 were the second-lowest level since that time. Falling apprehensions likely reflected fewer illegal inflows between 2006 and 2012, though the degree to which reduced inflows were a result of effective enforcement versus other factors like the recent U.S. economic downturn remains subject to debate (see "How Secure is the U.S. Border?").

The overwhelming majority of apprehensions take place along the Southwest border. In FY2014, the Border Patrol apprehended 479,377 aliens along this border, an increase of 64,980 from the previous year.[97] The majority of these apprehensions occurred in the Rio Grande Valley Sector (see discussion below).

Southwest Border Apprehensions by Sector

Figure 6 depicts apprehensions along the Southwest border for FY1992-FY2014, broken down by certain Border Patrol sectors. The sector-specific apprehension pattern generally adheres to the predictions of the 1994 National Strategic Plan. Increased enforcement in the El Paso and San Diego sectors was associated with high apprehensions in those sectors during the early 1990s, and then with falling apprehensions by the middle of the decade. Apprehensions in the San Diego and El Paso sectors remained well below their early-1990s levels throughout the following decade— findings that suggest border enforcement in those sectors has been broadly effective.

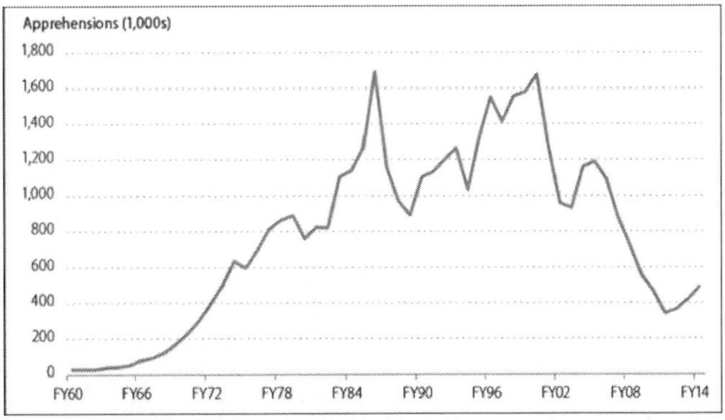

Source: FY1960-FY2012: CRS presentation of data provided by CBP Office of Congressional Affairs; FY2013- FY2014: U.S. Customs and Border Protection, Stats and Summaries, Nationwide Illegal Alien Apprehensions, Fiscal Years 1925-2014, http://www.cbp.gov/sites/default/files/documents/BP%20Total%20 Apps%20FY1925- FY2014_0.pdf.

Figure 5. Total USBP Apprehensions of Deportable Aliens, FY1960-FY2014.

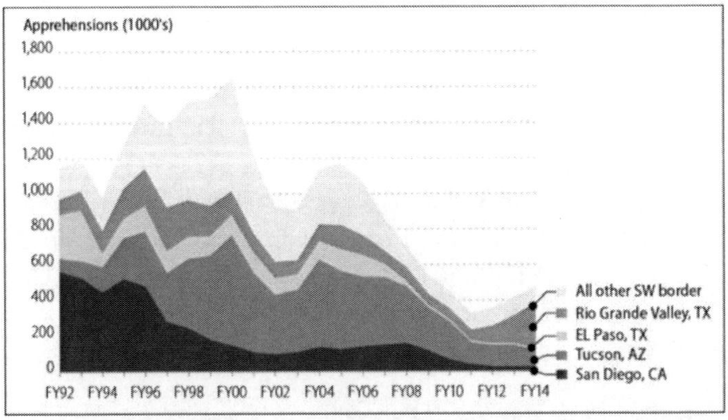

Source: FY1992-FY2012: CRS presentation of data provided by CBP Office of Congressional Affairs; FY2013- FY2014: U.S. Customs and Border Protection, Stats and Summaries, Southwest Border Sectors, Total Illegal Alien Apprehe-nsions by Fiscal Year, http://www.cbp.gov/sites/default/files/documents/ BP%20 Southwest%20Border%20Sector%20Apps%20FY1960%20-%20FY2014_0.pdf.

Figure 6. U.S. Border Patrol Apprehensions of Deportable Aliens, Southwest Border, by Selected Sectors, FY1992-FY2014.

Falling apprehensions in San Diego and El Paso during the late 1990s initially were more than offset by rising apprehensions in the Tucson, AZ, sector and other border locations, including the Laredo and Del Rio, TX, sectors. Since FY2011, apprehensions in Tucson have fallen back to their lowest level since 1993, but apprehensions in the Rio Grande Valley have increased, and now account for more than a quarter of Southwest border apprehensions.[98] Thus, since the initiation of the prevention through deterrence approach in the mid-1990s, it appears that success in San Diego and El Paso may have come at the expense of Tucson and other sectors.

Unique Subjects and Alien Recidivism

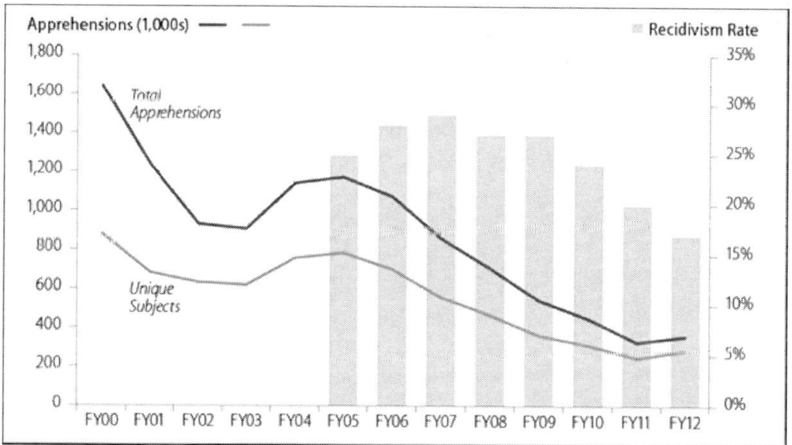

Source: CRS presentation of data provided by CBP Office of Congressional Affairs, March 10, 2013.

Notes: Total apprehensions refer to the total number of USBP apprehensions in Southwest border sectors; unique subjects refers to the number of different people apprehended based on biometric records. The recidivism rate is the percentage of unique individuals apprehended two or more times in a given fiscal year.

Figure 7. USBP Southwest Border Unique Subjects and Recidivism Rates (FY2000-FY2012).

Overall apprehensions data record apprehension *events*, and therefore count certain individuals more than once because they enter and are apprehended multiple times. Since 2000, the Border Patrol also has tracked the number of *unique subjects* the agency apprehends per year by analyzing biometric data (i.e., fingerprints and digital photographs) of persons apprehended.[99] As *Figure 7* illustrates, trends in unique subjects apprehended are similar to total apprehensions: falling from 2000-2003, climbing in 2004-2005, and then falling sharply from about 818,000 in 2005 to about 247,000 individuals in 2011, before climbing back to 284,000 in FY2012.[100]

Significantly, the gap between total and unique apprehensions has steadily narrowed, with unique subjects representing 54%-55% of total apprehensions in 2000-2001, 65%-70% in 2002-2010, and 75%-80% in 2011-2012. Put another way, each unique subject is being apprehended fewer times, on average, with the aggregate average number of apprehensions per person apprehended (i.e., total apprehensions divided by unique subjects) falling from 1.9 apprehensions per person in 2000 to 1.3 apprehensions per person in 2012.[101]

This trend is explained, in part, by the bars in *Figure 7*, which depict annual Southwest border recidivism rates, which USBP has tracked since 2005. The Border Patrol defines the annual recidivism rate as the percentage of unique subjects apprehended more than once in a given fiscal year. A goal of the Consequence Delivery System has been to deter aliens from re-entering—that is, to reduce recidivism. As *Figure 7* illustrates, recidivism rates increased slightly between 2005 (25%) and 2007 (29%), but have fallen since that time, reaching 17% in 2012.

Estimated "Got Aways" and "Turn Backs"

Border Patrol stations and sectors estimate the number of illegal entrants who successfully travel to the U.S. interior and who USBP ceased pursuing, or "got aways."[102] Stations and sectors also estimate "turn backs," the number of people who illegally cross the border but then cross back to Mexico. USBP uses the sum of got aways, turn backs, and apprehensions to estimate *the total number of known illegal entries* (also see "Border Patrol Effectiveness Rate"). The agency has used these data since 2006 to inform tactical decision making and to allocate resources across Southwest border sectors, but the Border Patrol has not published them or viewed them as reliable metrics of border security because of challenges associated with measuring got aways and turn backs across different border sectors.[103]

ADDITIONAL BORDER SECURITY DATA: MIGRANT SURVEYS

Apart from Border Patrol data on enforcement outcomes, a second major source of information about unauthorized migration and border security is survey data based on interviews with migrants and potential migrants. Much of the research on unauthorized migration across the Southwest border focuses on Mexicans because Mexico historically accounts for about 95% of persons apprehended at the Southwest border.[104] An advantage to surveys is that they may collect more information about their subjects than is found in enforcement data. In addition, because surveys are conducted within the U.S. interior as well as in migrant countries of origin (i.e., Mexico), surveys may capture more information about successful illegal inflows and about the deterrent effects of enforcement. In 2011, DHS commissioned a comprehensive study by the National Research Council (NRC) on the use of surveys and related methodologies to estimate the number of illegal U.S.-Mexico border crossings; and the NRC recommended that DHS use survey data along with enforcement data to measure illegal flows and the effectiveness of border enforcement.[105]

Two binational (U.S.-Mexican) surveys may be particularly useful for estimating illegal flows because they have examined migration dynamics in migrant-sending and –receiving communities for a number of years. The surveys are the Mexican Migration Field Research Program (MMFRP) based at the University of California-San Diego (UCSD) and the Mexican Migration Project (MMP) based at Princeton University. These targeted surveys ask a number of questions about U.S. immigration enforcement and how it affects respondents' migration histories and future plans. While analysts must account for the likelihood that unauthorized migrants may be less than forthcoming with interviewers and may be under-represented in certain survey samples, a body of social science research has made use of these data and developed commonly cited methodologies to account for these and other challenges.[106]

Probability of Apprehension

The UCSD and Princeton surveys both include data, based on self-reporting by people who have previously attempted to migrate illegally, on the probability that an alien will be apprehended on any given attempted crossing.

According to the Princeton data, the probability of being apprehended on any given crossing averaged about .37 in the two decades before IRCA's passage, ranging from a low of .31 to a high of .42 during this period. The probability of apprehension was somewhat lower in the decade after IRCA's passage, ranging from .22 to .32 between 1986 and 1995, and averaging .26 for the decade. Between 1996 and 2010, the last year for which sufficient data are available, the apprehension rate returned to an average of .36, with a low of .29 and a high of .50 during these years.[107]

The UCSD data suggest slightly higher apprehension rates, and show broadly similar trends. According to these data, the probability of being apprehended on any given crossing averaged .51 between 1974 and 1983, ranging from .32 to .67 during this period. After peaking at .67 in 1981, the probability of apprehension fell steadily to a low of .34 in 1992-1993. Since 1994 the probability of apprehension has averaged .49, ranging from .30 to .58 during this period.[108] The UCSD and the Princeton estimates of apprehension rates are substantially lower than the Border Patrol's current estimate, which is between .67 and .86.[109]

Border Deterrence

The Princeton and UCSD surveys thus find that unauthorized migrants are apprehended about a third to one-half of the time on any given crossing attempt. Both surveys also find that most aliens who attempt to cross illegally eventually succeed, meaning border deterrence rates are low. According to the Princeton data, between 75% and 90% of aliens apprehended at the border between 1965 and 2009 made a subsequent attempt to re-enter the United States and between 55% and 88% eventually succeeded. Border deterrence (i.e., the proportion of aliens who *failed* to re-enter the United States) averaged 37% in the two decades before IRCA's passage; averaged 26% between 1986 and 1995, reaching an all-time low of 21% in 1989; and averaged 34% in 1996-2009, the last year for which sufficient data are available. The UCSD survey finds at-theborder deterrence rates below 10% for the entire post-1980 period.[110]

Smuggling Fees

Princeton and UCSD surveys indicate that the majority of unauthorized migrants to the United States make use of human smugglers (often referred to in Mexico as "coyotes" or "polleros") to facilitate their illegal admission to the country. Indeed, whereas about 80% of unauthorized migrants from Mexico reportedly relied on human smugglers during the 1980s, about 90% did so in 2005-2007, though the use of smugglers may have declined a bit during the recent economic downturn.[111] Migrants' reliance on human smugglers, along with prices charged by smugglers, are an additional potential indicator of the effectiveness of U.S. border enforcement efforts, as more effective enforcement should increase the costs to smugglers of bringing migrants across the border, with smugglers passing such costs along to their clients in the form of higher fees.[112]

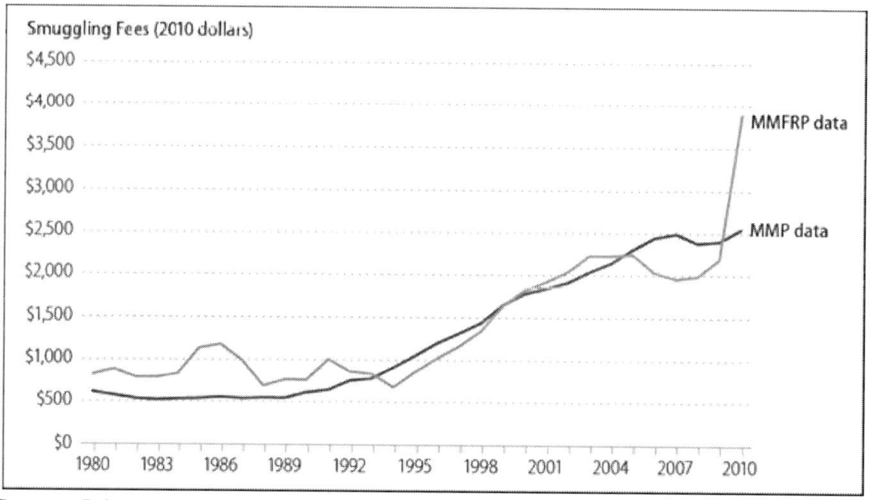

Source: Princeton University Mexican Migration Project (MMP) and University of California, San Diego Mexican Migration Field Research Program (MMFRP).

Notes: Data based on surveys of unauthorized Mexican migrants about their most recent unauthorized trip to the United States, with reported amounts adjusted for inflation using Bureau of Labor Statistics Consumer Price Index Research Series Using Current Methods (CPI-R-US). Data are a weighted three-year average to account for a small sample size. MMFRP estimate for 2010 may be unreliable due to a small sample size for that year.

Figure 8. Smuggling Fees Paid by Unauthorized Mexican Migrants, 1980-2010.

Figure 8 summarizes data from the Princeton and UCSD surveys describing average smuggling fees paid by certain unauthorized migrants from Mexico to the United States. In both cases, the data reflect reported smuggling fees based on surveys conducted with unauthorized migrants in the United States and in Mexico (i.e., after migrants had returned home), with fees adjusted for inflation and reported in 2010 dollars.

According to these data, smuggling fees were mostly flat between 1980 and 1993, at about $600- $850, with an average annual real growth rate of 1.5%-02.0%. Smuggling fees in both samples began to rise beginning around 1994, and climbed by an average of 11% per year between 1994 and 2002, reaching about $2,000 in both samples by 2002. Growth in smuggling fees has been slower since then, averaging 3.7% per year in the Princeton sample and 1.8% in the UCSD sample (excluding data from 2010, a year in which a small sample may have resulted in an unreliable annual estimate).[113] Thus, these data suggest that crossing the border illegally became somewhat more difficult—or at least most expensive—in the decade after the USBP began to implement its 1994 national strategy.

METRICS OF BORDER SECURITY

Some Members of Congress and others have asked the Border Patrol to provide a clear measure of how many aliens cross the border illegally and/or of the overall state of border security,[114] but measuring illegal border flows is difficult for the obvious reason that unauthorized aliens seek to avoid detection. While the Border Patrol has accurate data on various *enforcement outcomes*, these enforcement data were not designed to measure overall *illegal inflows*. Thus, DHS officials have testified that current enforcement data do not offer a suitable metric to describe border security.[115]

Apprehensions data are imperfect indicators of illegal flows because they exclude two important groups when it comes to unauthorized migration: aliens who successfully enter and remain in the United States (i.e., enforcement failures) and aliens who are deterred from entering the United States (i.e., certain enforcement successes). Thus, analysts do not know if a decline in apprehensions is an indicator of successful enforcement, because fewer people are attempting to enter, or of enforcement failures, because more of them are succeeding.[116] A further limitation to apprehensions data is that they count events, not unique individuals, so the same person may appear multiple times in the dataset after multiple entry attempts.

Unique apprehensions and USBP's estimate of got aways and turn backs are designed, in part, to address these limitations, but they offer only partial solutions. Unique apprehensions address the "overcount" problem associated with recidivism, but still misses information about certain enforcement failures (got-aways) and certain enforcement successes (deterrence). Estimated got aways and turn backs attempt to grapple with the latter problem; but (like apprehensions) they count events rather than individuals. Moreover, because estimated got-aways and turn backs attempt to measure enforcement outcomes that do not result in apprehensions, they are heavily dependent on the subjective judgment of individual border agents.[117] To the extent that agents—or the agency—are rewarded for effective enforcement, some people may question the credibility of a measure based on such judgments. Indeed, some media reports already have raised questions about the accuracy of the got away and turn back data.[118] The Border Patrol issued new guidance in September 2012 designed to impose greater consistency on turn back and got away data collection and reporting,[119] but data from the new system have not yet been analyzed.

A further limitation of enforcement data is that all such data depend on enforcement resources. In general, USBP enforcement outcomes (e.g., apprehensions, estimated got aways) are a function of (1) the underlying illegal flows and (2) the agency's ability to detect such flows. Enforcement data alone cannot disentangle these two factors. As a result, enforcement data may tend to overestimate illegal flows where resources are robust, and to under-estimate such flows where resources are scarce.

Given the limits of existing border enforcement data, DHS and outside researchers have developed several different metrics for estimating illegal border flows and describing border security. Three different methods for estimating illegal migration stocks and flows are described in the remainder of this section, and broad conclusions based on these metrics are described below (see "How Secure is the U.S. Border?").[120]

The Residual Method for Estimating Unauthorized Residents in the United States

Arguably the most well-developed approach to measuring unauthorized migration focuses on the number of unauthorized migrants residing in the United States. For many years, analysts within DHS and other social scientists have used the so-called "residual method" to estimate this number. In essence, the method involves using legal admissions data to estimate the legal, foreign-born population, and then subtracting this number from the overall count of foreign-born residents based on U.S. census data.[121]

The residual method provides limited information about the border *per se* because many unauthorized residents enter the United States through ports of entry, lawfully or otherwise.[122] Nonetheless, estimates of the size of the unauthorized population may offer several advantages over the border metrics discussed below. First, for many people, how many unauthorized aliens reside within the United States ultimately is a more important question than how many cross the border. After all, if illegal border flows fall to zero, but many people continue to enter illegally through ports of entry or by overstaying nonimmigrant visas, many people would consider such an outcome problematic. Second, for this reason, the size of the unauthorized population more comprehensively reflects how well immigration policy and immigration enforcement function, including for example the effectiveness of worksite and other interior enforcement efforts as well as how well visas meet employer and family demands. Third, estimates of the unauthorized population offer the advantage of a nearly 30-year track record and a relatively uncontroversial methodology. As long ago as 2001, the Department of Justice used the total estimated stock of unauthorized migrants in the United States as a key performance metric for the department's evaluation of its border security efforts.[123]

CBP Metrics of Border Security

Operational Control of the Border

Section 2 of the Secure Fence Act of 2006 (P.L. 109-367) defines operational control of the border to mean "the prevention of all unlawful entries into the United States, including entries by terrorists, other unlawful aliens, instruments of terrorism, narcotics, and other contraband." Most experts agree that preventing 100% of unlawful entries across U.S. borders is an impossible task;[124] and through FY2010, the Border Patrol classified portions of the border as being under "effective" or "operational" control if the agency "has the ability to detect, respond, and interdict illegal activity at the border or after entry into the United States."[125] The agency conducted a five-level assessment of border security, with the two top levels ("controlled" and "managed") defined as being under effective control, and the three remaining levels ("monitored," "low-level monitored," and "remote/low activity") defined as not being under effective control.[126] In February 2010, the Border

Patrol reported that 1,107 miles (57%) of the Southwest border were under effective control.[127]

Beginning in FY2011, USBP stopped using this measure of effective control.[128] The agency reportedly no longer views operational or effective control as a useful metric because station and sector chiefs could not accurately and reliably use the five-level coding scheme to assess different border regions.[129] In addition, given the dynamic nature of border threats, the agency does not view it as useful to evaluate border security on a mile-by-mile basis.[130]

Border Conditions Index

In May 2011, DHS announced that CBP was developing a new "border conditions index" (BCI).[131] Reportedly, the BCI will include measures of estimated illegal flows between ports of entry, wait times and the efficiency of legal flows at ports of entry, and public safety and quality of life in border regions. These three components will be combined to develop a holistic "score" calculated for different regions of the border.[132] With these different components, the BCI includes some of the same information some Members of Congress and others may consider to be of interest with respect to describing border security, but DHS officials have emphasized that the BCI encompasses a broader set of issues than "border security" as this term is normally used, and that the BCI therefore may not satisfy demands for a single comprehensive measure of border security.[133] Officials have also testified that the BCI remains in the development phase.[134]

Border Patrol Effectiveness Rate

By dividing apprehensions and estimated turn backs (i.e., successful enforcement outcomes) by estimated known illegal entries (see "Estimated "Got Aways" and "Turn Backs""), USBP calculates an *estimated enforcement effectiveness rate*. Some people have proposed using this effectiveness rate as a measure of border security. While using enforcement data to measure border security raises a number of methodological concerns (see "Metrics of Border Security"), the effectiveness *rate* would have an advantage over other enforcement metrics because, as a ratio, it may be somewhat less sensitive to the level of enforcement resources in place.[135] As with the BCI, it is difficult to evaluate USBP's effectiveness rate as a border metric because little is known about the agency's new protocols for collecting got away and turn back data.

Estimating Illegal Flows Using Recidivism Data

For many years, social scientists have used the so-called "capture-recapture" method to estimate unauthorized flows based on recidivism data.[136] The capture-recapture method estimates the total flow of unauthorized migrants based on the ratio of persons re-apprehended after an initial enforcement action to the total number of persons apprehended.[137] In the basic model, the probability of apprehension is calculated by taking the ratio of recidivist apprehensions to total apprehensions; and the total illegal inflow is calculated by dividing total apprehensions by the odds of apprehension.[138] See *Appendix* for more details.

An advantage to the capture-recapture method is that it relies on observable administrative enforcement data—apprehensions and recidivists—to calculate key border security metrics: apprehension rates and illegal flows. Yet the basic model assumes that all intending unauthorized migrants eventually succeed (i.e., that none are deterred at the border).[139] To the extent that the build-up in border enforcement resources and the deployment of the Consequence Delivery System cause some would-be unauthorized migrants to give up and return home, the capture-recapture method *underestimates* successful enforcement and *overestimates* illegal flows. Likewise, the basic model assumes that all border crossers originate in—and are repatriated to— Mexico, facilitating re-entry attempts. As the proportion of border crossers from countries other than Mexico increases—as it has in recent years[140]—repatriated aliens may be less likely to attempt re-entry, an additional reason the capture-recapture model may over-estimate illegal inflows.

Thus, to estimate illegal flows based on the capture-recapture method, enforcement data on apprehensions and repeat apprehensions must be supplemented with additional information about the proportion of migrants deterred, and must control for lower recidivism rates among nonMexicans.[141] Estimates of illegal flows based on this methodology are discussed below (see "How Secure is the U.S. Border?").

How Secure Is the U.S. Border?

While no single metric accurately and reliably describes border security (see "Metrics of Border Security"), most analysts agree, based on available data, that the number of illegal border crossers fell sharply between about 2005 and 2011, with some rise in illegal flows in 2012. This conclusion is supported by key Border Patrol enforcement data described above, including the drop in total apprehensions, the drop in unique apprehensions, and the drop in estimated got aways and total estimated known entries across eight out of nine Border Patrol sectors.

Survey data confirm an apparent drop in illegal inflows, and measure such effects away from the border. For example, according to data collected by the Princeton Mexican Migration Project, an average of about 2% of all Mexican men initiated a first unauthorized trip to the United States each year between 1973 and 2002; but that percentage has fallen sharply since 2002, to below 0.4% in 2008-2011.[142] Estimates of the unauthorized population based on the residual method report drops of about 1 million unauthorized migrants living in the United States, from about 12.4 million in 2007 to 13.1 million in 2011.[143] And the Pew Hispanic Center estimates that net (i.e., northbound minus southbound) unauthorized migration from Mexico fell to about zero in 2011, and that outflows may have even exceeded inflows.[144]

According to GAO's analysis of Border Patrol metrics, eight out of nine Border Patrol sectors (all except the Big Bend sector) showed improved effectiveness rates between FY2006 and FY2011.[145] In the Tucson sector, the main focus of GAO's analysis, the effectiveness rate improved from 67% to 87% during this period. The San Diego, El Centro, Yuma, and El Paso sectors all had effectiveness rates in FY2011 of about 90%; the Del Rio and Laredo sectors (along with Tucson) had rates above 80%; and the Big Bend and Rio Grande Valley sectors had rates between 60% and 70%.

CRS estimates based on USBP recidivism data and using the capture-recapture method also suggest that illegal flows between ports of entry fell substantially between 2005 and 2011, before rising somewhat in 2012 (see *Figure 9*). The shaded area in *Figure 9* depicts total estimated illegal inflows, which are equal to the total number of apprehensions divided by the estimated odds of successful enforcement (See *Appendix* for a discussion of the methodology used to generate *Figure 9*). Based on available data, the figure assumes deterrence rates in 2000-2012 were between 20% (the estimates depicted by the upper bound of the shaded area) and 40% (the lower bound). As the figure indicates, total estimated illegal inflows fell from a high of between 760,000 and 1.4 million in 2004 to a low of between 340,000 and 580,000 in 2009-2010.[146] The model estimates that total illegal inflows were between 400,000 and 660,000 in 2012. Although recidivism data are not available to make similar calculations for previous years, apprehension levels and survey data from the 1980s and 1990s suggest that total illegal inflows likely were lower in 2007-2012 than at any other point in the last three decades.

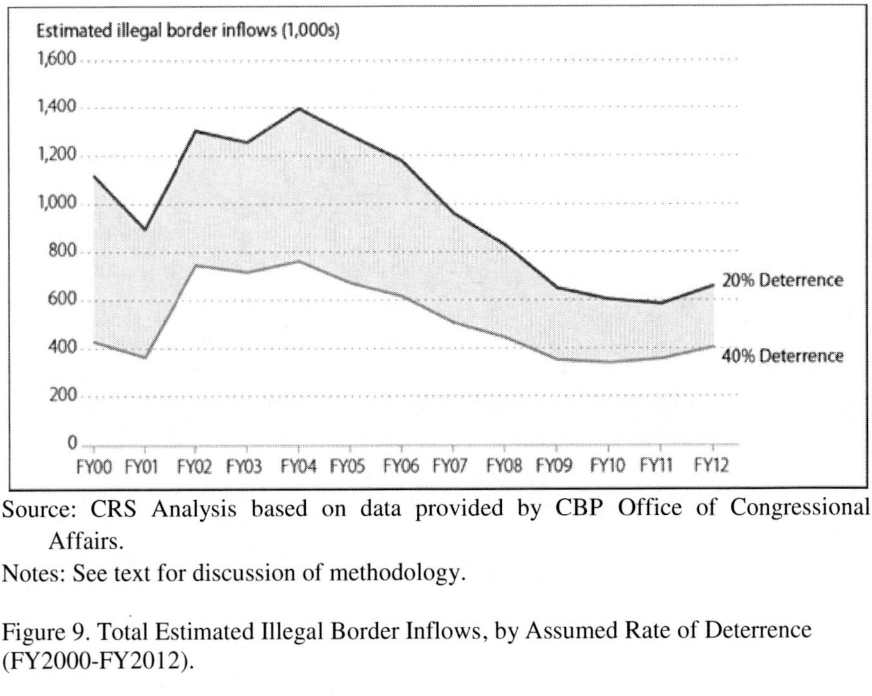

Source: CRS Analysis based on data provided by CBP Office of Congressional Affairs.

Notes: See text for discussion of methodology.

Figure 9. Total Estimated Illegal Border Inflows, by Assumed Rate of Deterrence (FY2000-FY2012).

Border enforcement is only one of several factors that affect illegal migration.[147] Thus, if illegal entries indeed fell after 2006, to what degree is this change attributable to enforcement versus other developments, such as the U.S. economic downturn since 2007, and/or economic and demographic changes in Mexico and other countries of origin?[148] Disentangling the effects of enforcement from other factors influencing migration flows is particularly difficult in the current case because many of the most significant new enforcement efforts—including a sizeable share of new border enforcement personnel, most border fencing, new enforcement practices at the border, and many of the new migration enforcement measures within the United States—all have occurred at the same time as the most severe recession since the 1930s.

Nonetheless, the drop in recidivism rates suggests that an increasing proportion of aliens are being deterred by CBP's enforcement efforts, a finding that also appears to be reflected in survey data from the Princeton survey (see "Border Deterrence"). Surveys of unauthorized migrants repatriated to Mexico in 2005 and 2010 also suggest that enforcement is increasingly likely to deter future immigration.[149] As *Figure 9* illustrates, the more unauthorized migrants that are being deterred by U.S. enforcement efforts, the lower the number of successful illegal inflows.

Academic research from 2012 also provides evidence that border enforcement has contributed to a reduction in illegal flows.[150] These findings are noteworthy, in part, because they contradict earlier academic research, much of which found that border enforcement had a limited impact or even was counter-productive when it came to migration control efforts (also see "Migration Flows: "Caging" Effects and Alternative Modes of Entry").[151] This research suggests that the recent build-up in immigration enforcement at the border and within the United States may have had a greater deterrent effect on illegal migration than earlier efforts.[152] Nonetheless, some uncertainty will remain about the true level of border security as long as U.S. employment demand remains below historic levels.

Unintended and Secondary Consequences of Border Enforcement

The preceding discussion includes estimates of what may be described as the primary costs and benefits of border enforcement, defined in terms of congressional appropriations and deployment of enforcement resources on one hand, and alien apprehensions and other indicators of successful enforcement on the other. A comprehensive analysis of the costs and benefits of border enforcement policies may also consider possible unintended and secondary consequences. Such consequences may produce both costs and benefits—many of which are difficult to measure—in at least five areas: border-area crime and migrant deaths, migrant flows, environmental impacts, effects on border communities, and U.S. foreign relations.

Border-Area Crime and Migrant Deaths

Illegal border crossing is associated with a certain level of border crime and violence and, in the most unfortunate cases, with deaths of illegal border crossers and border-area law enforcement officers. Unauthorized migration may be associated with crime and mortality in several distinct ways. First, unauthorized migration is associated with crime—apart from the crime of illegal entry—because some unauthorized migrants contract with immigrant smugglers and because unauthorized migrants may engage in related illegal activity, such as document fraud. Yet fear of the police may make unauthorized aliens *less* likely to engage in other types of criminal activity, and research on the subject finds low immigrant criminality rates, especially when accounting for education levels and other demographic characteristics.[153] Second, illegal border crossers face risks associated with crossing the border at dangerous locations, where they may die from exposure or from drowning.[154]

Border *enforcement* therefore may affect crime and migrant mortality in complex ways.[155] On one hand, the concentration of enforcement resources around the border may exacerbate adverse outcomes by making migrants more likely to rely on smugglers, as noted above (see "Smuggling Fees"). The 1994 National Strategic Plan *predicted* a short-term rise in border violence for these reasons.[156] On the other hand, to the extent that enforcement successfully deters illegal crossers, such prevention should reduce crime and mortality. The concentration of law enforcement personnel near the border may further enhance public safety and migrant protection, especially where CBP has made a priority of protecting vulnerable populations.[157]

The empirical record suggests that there is *no significant difference* in the average violent crime rate in border and non-border metropolitan areas.[158] Indeed, the border cities El Paso, TX, and San Diego, CA, are regularly listed among the safest large cities in the country based on their rankings among similarly sized cities in the Federal Bureau of Investigation's Uniform Crime Report.[159] The specific impact of border enforcement on border-area crime is unknown, however, because available data cannot separate the influence of border enforcement from other factors.[160]

With respect to mortality, available data about migrant deaths along the Southwest border are presented in *Figure 10*. The figures come from academic research based on local medical investigators' and examiners' offices in California, Arizona, New Mexico, and Texas between 1985 and 1998 (the University of Houston's Center for Immigration Research, CIR); Mexican foreign ministry and Mexican media counts compiled by the American Civil Liberties Union of San Diego; and data compiled by DHS based on bodies recovered on the U.S. side of the border.[161] All three data sources reflect *known* migrant deaths, and therefore undercount actual migrant deaths since some bodies may not be discovered.[162] Additionally, U.S. data sources generally do not include information from the Mexican side of the border and therefore further undercount migration-related fatalities.

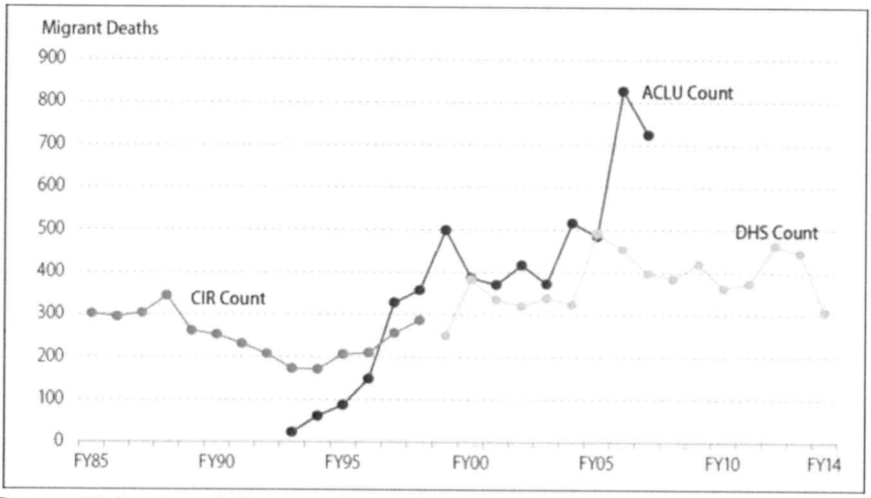

Source: University of Houston Center for Immigration Research (CIR); Jimenez, "Humanitarian Crisis," 2009 (ACLU); CBP Office of Congressional Affairs and U.S. Customs and Border Protection, Stats and Summaries, Southwest Border Deaths by Fiscal Year, http://www.cbp.gov/sites/default/files/documents/BP%20Southwest%20Border%20Sector%20Deaths%20FY1998%20-%20FY2014_0.pdf.

Figure 10. Known Migrant Deaths, Southwest Border, 1985-2014.

As *Figure 10* illustrates, data from the CIR indicate that known migrant deaths fell from a high of 344 in 1988 to a low of 171 in 1994 before climbing back to 286 in 1998. According to DHS data, known migrant deaths climbed from 250 in 1999 to 492 in 2005, and averaged 431 deaths per year in 2005-2009. DHS's count fell to an average of 369 per year in 2010-2011, but increased to 463 in FY2012 before falling again to 445 in FY2013 and to a low of 307 in FY2014.

The ACLU found that known migrant deaths increased from just 80 per year in 1993-1996 to 496 per year in 1997-2007. The apparent increase in migrant deaths in the past decades is noteworthy in light of the apparent decline in unauthorized entries during the same period. These data offer evidence that border crossings have become more hazardous since the "prevention through deterrence" policy went into effect in the 1990s,[163] though (as with crime) the precise impact of enforcement on migrant deaths is unknown.

Migration Flows: "Caging" Effects and Alternative Modes of Entry

With illegal border crossing becoming more dangerous and more expensive, some unauthorized aliens appear to have adapted their behavior to avoid crossing the border via traditional pathways. Most notably, social science research suggests that border enforcement has had the unintended consequence of encouraging unauthorized aliens to settle permanently in the United States rather than working temporarily and then returning home, as was more common prior to the mid-1980s.[164] The primary evidence for this so-called "caging" effect is that unauthorized migrants appear to be staying longer in the United States and raising families here more often rather than making regular trips to visit families that remain in countries of origin.[165] Although other factors also likely contribute to these changes,[166] survey results appear to confirm that border enforcement has been a factor behind these longer stays.[167]

A second unintended consequence of enhanced border enforcement between ports of entry may have been an increase in illegal entries through ports of entry and other means. According to UCSD Mexico Migration Field Research Program research, unauthorized Mexican migrants from one community in Mexico interviewed in 2009 used six different methods to enter the United States illegally, with one in four such aliens passing illegally through a port of entry by using borrowed or fraudulent documents or by hiding in a vehicle.[168] Based on three different surveys conducted between 2008 and 2010, UCSD researchers found that the probability of being apprehended while passing illegally though a port of entry was about half as high as the probability of being apprehended while crossing between the ports.[169] CBP's Passenger Compliance Examination (COMPEX) System reportedly detects very little illegal migration through ports of entry, however.[170] There is also anecdotal evidence that unauthorized aliens have recently turned to maritime routes as alternative strategies to cross the U.S.-Mexican border.[171]

Environmental Impact

A third set of potential unintended consequences concern the effect of border enforcement on the environment. As with the effects of enforcement on border crime and violence, the effects of enforcement on the environment are complex because they reflect changes in migrant behavior and the secondary effects of enforcement per se.

On one hand, many illegal border crossers transit through sensitive environmental areas, cutting vegetation for shelter and fire, potentially causing wildfires, increasing erosion through repeated use of trails, and discarding trash.[172] Thus, to the extent that border enforcement successfully deters illegal flows, enforcement benefits the environment by reducing these undesirable outcomes. On the other hand, the construction of fencing, roads, and other tactical infrastructure may damage border-area ecosystems. These environmental considerations may be especially important because much of the border runs through remote and environmentally sensitive areas.[173] For this reason, even when accounting for the possible environmental benefits of reduced illegal border flows, some environmental groups have opposed border infrastructure projects because they threaten rare and endangered species as well as other wildlife by damaging ecosystems and restricting the movement of animals, and because surveillance towers and artificial night lighting have detrimental effects on migrant birds.[174]

Effects on Border Communities and Civil Rights

Although economists disagree about the overall economic impact of unauthorized migration, unauthorized migrants may impose a number of costs at the local level, including through their use of schools and other public programs.[175] Some are also concerned that illegal migration undermines the rule of law. For these reasons, successful border enforcement may benefit border communities by reducing illegal inflows.

Yet some business owners on the Southwest and Northern borders have complained that certain border enforcement efforts threaten their economic activities, including farming and ranching activities that are disrupted by the deployment of USBP resources to the border and commercial activities that suffer from reduced regional economic activity.[176] More generally, some people have complained that the construction of barriers divides communities that have straddled international land borders for generations.[177]

Some people have raised additional concerns about the effects of border enforcement on civil rights. Some residents of Southwest and Northern border communities see enhanced border enforcement as leading to racial profiling and wrongful detentions.[178] On top of this general concern, some people argue that Operation Streamline raises additional questions about whether migrants receive adequate legal protections during fast-tracked criminal procedures.[179] And some have argued that mistreatment and abuse are widespread in CBP detention facilities.[180]

An additional concern that some have raised about CBP's focus on high consequence enforcement is the possibility that focusing scarce judicial and prosecutorial resources on immigration enforcement diverts attention from more serious crimes.[181] A 2013 Justice Department study found that the number of immigration defendants in federal courts increased 664% between 1995 and 2010 (from 5,103 to 39,001); and that immigration cases accounted for 60% of the overall increase in pretrial detentions during that period.[182] More generally, immigration offenders accounted for 46% of federal arrests in 2010, outnumbering all other crimes and up from 22% a decade earlier.[183] A 2008 study by the Administrative Office of the U.S. Courts found that while Congress had provided short-term funding to allow the courts to respond to increased prosecutions, the courts faced a shortage of suitable courthouse and detention facilities in some border locations.[184]

Effects on Regional Relations

What are the effects of U.S. border enforcement policies on U.S. relations with its continental neighbors, Mexico and Canada? The United States and Canada have a strong record of collaborative border enforcement, including through 15 binational, multi-agency Integrated Border Enforcement Teams (IBETs) operating at 24 locations at and between U.S.-Canadian ports of entry. In February 2011, President Obama and Prime Minister Harper signed the Beyond the Border declaration, which described their shared visions for a common approach to perimeter security and economic competitiveness; and the countries released an Action Plan on December 7, 2011, to implement the agreement.[185] While some Canadians have raised objections to some of the information sharing and joint law enforcement provisions of the agreement,[186] border enforcement between the ports has not been identified as a significant source of bilateral tension.

The United States and Mexico also cooperate extensively on border enforcement operations at the Southwest border.[187] Yet immigration enforcement occasionally has been a source of bilateral tension. And with Mexicans being the most frequent target of U.S. immigration enforcement efforts, some Mexicans have expressed concerns about the construction of border fencing, the effects of border enforcement on migrant deaths, and the protection of unaccompanied minors and other vulnerable groups, among other issues related to immigration enforcement.[188]

Conclusion: Understanding the Costs and Benefits of Border Enforcement between Ports of Entry

The United States has focused substantial resources along its land borders to prevent and control illegal migration since the 1980s, with investments in personnel, fencing, and surveillance assets all up significantly in the post 9/11 period, in particular. Since 2005, CBP also has transformed its approach to managing enforcement outcomes, through its Consequence Delivery System.

Measuring the *effects* of border enforcement is difficult. On one hand, after reaching a high point in 2000, Border Patrol apprehensions fell sharply in 2007-2011, reaching a 42-year low in FY2011. The Border Patrol's IDENT database also indicates a declining proportion of aliens is apprehended more than once (i.e., recidivism is down). Estimates based on enforcement and survey data and accounting for estimated apprehension and deterrence rates suggest that total illegal inflows in 2009-2011 were well below levels observed in the two decades after IRCA's passage, but that illegal inflows increased somewhat in 2012.

On the other hand, there is also some evidence that migrants have adapted to more difficult conditions at the border by using other means to enter the United States and by remaining longer. A comprehensive accounting also may consider various potential unintended consequences of border enforcement on the civil rights of legal residents and U.S. citizens in the border region, on migrants' human rights, on the quality of life in border communities, on the environment and wildlife, and on U.S.-regional relations.

What do these findings mean for Members of Congress who oversee border security and immigration policy? Especially in light of current fiscal constraints, some Members of Congress may evaluate future border enforcement in terms of expected returns on America's investments, and they may consider the possibility that certain additional investments at the border may be met with diminishing returns. Border infrastructure may offer an example: with 651 miles of fencing and barriers already in place along the Southwest border, each additional mile would be in ever more remote locations, and therefore more expensive to install and maintain and likely to deter fewer unauthorized migrants. Similarly, some Members of Congress may question the concrete benefits of deploying more sophisticated surveillance systems across the entire northern and southern borders, including vast regions in which too few personnel are deployed to respond to the occasional illegal entry that may be detected.

Deciding how to allocate border resources therefore requires a clear definition of the goals of border security. Zero admissions of unauthorized migrants may not be a realistic goal when it comes to migration control, as noted above, and is a higher standard than is expected of most law enforcement agencies. While this report focuses on migration control at U.S. borders, border security also encompasses the detection and interdiction of weapons of mass destruction (WMD), narcotics, and other illicit goods; policies to combat human trafficking; and other security goals. These diverse goals are often conflated in an undifferentiated debate about "border security"; but each of these goals may suggest a different mix of border investments, as well as different metrics and different standards for successful enforcement outcomes. Should policies to prevent unauthorized migration be held to the same standards as policies to prevent the entry of WMDs, for example?

Regardless of how these questions are answered in principle, debates about immigration control and border security may benefit from better metrics of border security and illegal migration, and from a more analytical approach to program design. The Border Patrol has taken a step in this direction by analyzing recidivism data as a function of different enforcement outcomes through its Consequence Delivery System. This report also identifies several metrics for measuring border security, all of which have advantages and disadvantages. In the context of immigration policy and a possible immigration reform bill, Members of Congress may choose to focus on the total number of unauthorized aliens in the United States, in addition to border flows, since border enforcement is just one of many factors (along with interior enforcement, visa policies, etc.) influencing the size of the unauthorized population, and because more is known about the population number than about border flows.

APPENDIX. CAPTURE-RECAPTURE METHODOLOGY

The capture-recapture methodology for estimating unauthorized migration flows based on total and recidivist alien apprehensions was first proposed by the sociologist Thomas Espenshade in 1995.[189] Espenshade's original model assumed that all intending migrants (i.e., everyone who makes an initial crossing attempt) eventually succeed—an assumption supported by academic research at the time.[190] Likewise, the model focused exclusively on unauthorized Mexican migrants, a population of particular interest since Mexicans represented 96% of all alien apprehensions during the 1990s,[191] and since Mexico's long shared border with the United States creates unique enforcement dynamics, including high recidivism rates.

The basic capture-recapture model works backwards from the total number of apprehensions and recidivist apprehensions to calculate total illegal flow and the odds of apprehension. First, by definition, the number of apprehensions is related to the total number of illegal crossings multiplied by the probability of being apprehended on any given attempt. For example, if 1,000 aliens attempt to cross, and the probability of being apprehended on a given trip is 50%, then the number of apprehensions would be 500. If unsuccessful migrants always make a second (and subsequent) attempt to enter, the number of aliens making a second attempt is equal to number of initial apprehensions (i.e., 500 in the previous example); and the number of apprehensions among one-time repeat crossers would be 250. In the following period, 250 would attempt entry and 125 would succeed, and so on. By adding up these iterations, Espenshade shows that the total number of apprehensions (A) is equal to the total flow of unauthorized aliens (F) times the odds of apprehension, where odds are defined statistically as the probability of apprehension (P) divided by one minus the probability of apprehension.[192] Re-arranging this statement to solve for flow:

$$F = A/[P/(1-P)] \tag{1}$$

Second, the ratio of repeat apprehensions to total apprehensions is used to calculate the probability of apprehension on a given attempt. In short, the formula for repeat apprehensions is simply the formula for total apprehensions times the probability of being apprehended. As a result, repeat apprehensions (R) divided by total apprehensions (A) yields the probability of apprehension ($P_{\text{apprenehsion}}$) on a given trip:[193]

$$P_{\text{apprenehsion}} = R/A \tag{2}$$

The methodology used in this report adapts Espenshade's model to account for the fact that some aliens do not make a second or subsequent attempt after being apprehended—that is, that some are deterred.[194] This modified capture-recapture model also has been used in a 2013 Council on Foreign Relations report;[195] and DHS officials have indicated that DHS's Border Conditions Index, now under development, employs a similar method to estimate illegal flows between ports of entry.[196] In the modified model, the estimated probability of apprehension defined in equation (2) is divided by one minus the probability of deterrence to calculate the probability of successful enforcement (Penforcemenj:

$$P_{enforcement} = (R/A)/(1\text{-}D) \qquad (3)$$

Figure 9 in this report was generated by using equation (3) to estimate the probability of successful enforcement at the Southwest border and equation (1) to estimate total Southwest border illegal flows. In the absence of country-specific recidivism rates (and in light of the higher costs to reentry following deportation of non-Mexicans), CRS's analysis assumes non-Mexicans do not re-enter in the same fiscal year. Thus, the calculations for equation (3) use CBP data on total recidivists divided by CBP data on Mexican apprehensions to calculate a Mexico-specific apprehension rate.[197] Based on available survey and USBP turn back data, deterrence rates were assumed to fall between 20 and 40%. CRS further assumed that Mexican and non-Mexican aliens are apprehended at the same rate, and thus uses the value of P calculated in equation (3), along with CBP data on total Southwest border apprehensions, to estimate total Southwest border illegal inflows based on equation (1).

End Notes

[1] The Bracero program was a formal guest worker program managed jointly by the United States and Mexico that admitted about 4.6 million workers between 1942 and 1964.

[2] The estimated population of unauthorized aliens was about 1.7 million by 1979 and about 3.2 million in 1986; most researchers, however, consider earlier estimates of the unauthorized population to be unreliable. See Jennifer Van Hook and Frank D. Bean, "Estimating Unauthorized Mexican Migration to the United States: Issues and Trends," in Binational Study: Migration Between Mexico and the United States (Washington, DC: US Commission on Immigration Reform, 1998), pp. 538-540.

[3] Except as otherwise noted, this report focuses exclusively on border security as it relates to the prevention of unauthorized migration. On the relationship among unauthorized migration, illegal drugs and other contraband, international terrorists, and other types of border threats, see CRS Report R42969, Border Security: Understanding Threats at U.S. Borders, by Jerome P. Bjelopera and Kristin Finklea.

[4] See archived CRS Report RL33874, Unauthorized Aliens Residing in the United States: Estimates Since 1986, by Ruth Ellen Wasem.

[5] See CRS Report R42988, U.S. Immigration Policy: Chart Book of Key Trends, by William A. Kandel.

[6] Department of Homeland Security press release, remarks by Secretary of Homeland Security Jeh Johnson (and accompanying slides), "Border Security in the 21st Century," October 9, 2014 (Hereafter referred to as "Border Security in the 21st Century"). The spike in apprehensions in FY2014 can be largely attributed to the unaccompanied alien children crisis. See CRS Report R43599, Unaccompanied Alien Children: An Overview.

[7] See DHS "Fixing Our Immigration Broken System Through Executive Action – Key Facts" at http://www.dhs.gov/ immigration-action?utm_source=hp_feature&utm_medium=web& utm_campaign=dhs_hp.

[8] Led by Texas, 17 states have moved to sue President Obama over his executive action on immigration. "17 States Suing on Immigration." The New York Times, December 3, 2014, http://www.nytimes.com/2014/12/04/us/executiveaction-on-immigration-prompts-texas-to-sue.html?_r=0.

[9] See, for example, Alan Gomez, "Border Security Quandary Could Kill Immigration Bill," USA Today, April 2, 2013.

[10] Act of May 28, 1924; (43 Stat. 240).

[11] Immigration Act of May 26, 1924 (43 Stat. 153).

[12] See U.S. Customs and Border Protection (CBP), "Border Patrol History," http://www. cbp.gov/xp/cgov/ border_security/border_patrol/border_patrol_ohs/history.xml.

[13] See Kitty Calavita, Inside the State: The Bracero Program, Immigration, and the I.N.S. (New York: Routledge, 1992); Mark Reisler, By the Sweat of Their Brow: Mexican Immigrant Labor in the United States, 1900-1940 (Westport, CT: Greenwood Press, 1976); Douglas S. Massey, Jorge Durand, and Nolan J. Malone, Beyond Smoke and Mirrors: Mexican Immigration in an Era of Economic Integration (New York: Russell Sage Foundation, 2002).

[14] See CRS Report R42560, Mexican Migration to the United States: Policy and Trends, coordinated by Ruth Ellen Wasem. Legislative changes included the termination of the U.S. Mexican Bracero guest worker program in 1965 and the imposition of numeric limits on migration from Mexico and other Western Hemisphere countries pursuant to the Immigration and Nationality Act Amendments of 1965 (P.L. 89-236).

[15] See U.S. Congress, House Committee on the Judiciary, The "Immigration Reform and Control Act of 1986" (P.L. 99-603), 99th Cong., 2nd Sess., December 1986, H. Rept. 99-14 (Washington: GPO, 1986).

[16] The seven laws that included border-related provisions were the Immigration Act of 1990 (P.L. 101-649), the Illegal Immigration Reform and Immigrant Responsibility Act of 1996 (P.L. 104-208, Div. C), the USA-PATRIOT Act of 2002 (P.L. 107-56), the Homeland Security Act of 2002 (P.L. 107-296), the Intelligence Reform and Terrorism Prevention Act of 2004 (108-458), the REAL-ID Act of 2005 (P.L. 109-13, Div. B), and the Secure Fence Act of 2006 (P.L. 109-367).

[17] U.S. Office of National Drug Control Policy, National Drug Control Strategy: Reclaiming Our Communities from Drugs and Violence (Washington, DC: U.S. Department of Justice, 1994), https://www.ncjrs.gov/pdffiles1/ondcp/ 150489.pdf.

[18] U.S. Border Patrol, Border Patrol Strategic Plan: 1994 and Beyond, July 1994, pp. 6-7 (Hereinafter, National Strategic Plan).

[19] The Automated Biometric Identification (IDENT) system is DHS's primary biometric database. Certain aliens' biometric records are added to IDENT upon admission to the

United States, when aliens are apprehended or arrested by a DHS agency, and when aliens apply for certain immigration benefits.

[20] National Strategic Plan, pp. 9-10.

[21] U.S. General Accountability Office, Illegal Immigration: Southwest Border Strategy Results Inconclusive; More Evaluation Needed, GAO/GGD-98-21, December 1997.

[22] U.S. Congress, Senate Committee on Appropriations, Departments of Commerce, Justice, and State, The Judiciary, and Related Agencies Appropriations Bill, 1996, report to accompany H.R. 2076, 104th Cong., 1st sess., S.Rept. 104- 139 and U.S. Congress, House Committee on Appropriations, Making Appropriations for the Departments of Commerce, Justice, and State, The Judiciary, and Related Agencies For the Fiscal Year Ending September 30, 1996, and for Other Purposes, report to accompany H.R. 2076, 104th Cong., 1st sess., H.Rept. 104-378.

[23] P.L. 104-208, Div. C §102.

[24] Department of Homeland Security, Bureau of Customs and Border Protection, National Border Patrol Strategy, March 1, 2005. Hereinafter, USBP National Strategy.

[25] USBP National Strategy, p. 3. This definition differs from the statutory definition found in Section 2 of the Secure Fence Act of 2006 (P.L. 109-367); see in this report "Operational Control of the Border."

[26] CBP, 2012-2016 Border Patrol Strategic Plan, Washington, DC: 2012, p. 7.

[27] Ibid.

[28] DHS, "Fact Sheet: Secure Border Initiative," https://www.hsdl.org/?view&did=440470.

[29] Ibid.

[30] Prior to 1996, the INA included distinct provisions for the "exclusion" of inadmissible aliens and the "deportation" of certain aliens from within the United States. Pursuant to §§301-309 of the Illegal Immigration Reform and Immigrant Responsibility Act of 1996 (IIRIRA, P.L. 104-208, Div. C), deportation and exclusion proceedings were combined into a unified "removal" proceeding (8 U.S.C. 1229a). This report uses "deportation" to refer to the compulsory return of aliens to their country of origin prior to the implementation of IIRIRA in 1997, and "removal" to refer to aliens returned under these provisions since 1997.

[31] DHS estimated that there were 623,292 alien "absconders" in August 2006, many of whom had failed to appear for removal hearings after being apprehended at the border; see Doris Meissner and Donald Kerwin, DHS and Immigration: Taking Stock and Correcting Course, Migration Policy Institute, Washington, DC, February 2009, p. 44, http://www.migrationpolicy.org/pubs/DHS_Feb09.pdf.

[32] DHS, "Fact Sheet: Secure Border Initiative," https://www.hsdl.org/?view&did=440470.

[33] CBP, "DHS Secretary Announces End to 'Catch and Release' on Southern Border," http://www.cbp.gov/xp/cgov/ admin/c1_archive/messages/end_catch_release.xml.

[34] DHS, "Fact Sheet: Secure Border Initiative," https://www.hsdl.org/?view&did=440470.

[35] Ibid.

[36] Ibid. Interior enforcement programs are not discussed in this report; see CRS Report R42057, Interior Immigration Enforcement: Programs Targeting Criminal Aliens, by Marc R. Rosenblum and William A. Kandel; and CRS Report R40002, Immigration-Related Worksite Enforcement: Performance Measures, by Andorra Bruno.

[37] Section 240B of the INA permits immigration agents and judges to allow certain removable aliens to "voluntarily depart" the United States. In contrast with aliens subject to formal removal, aliens subject to voluntary departure generally do not face additional immigration-related penalties.

[38] Pursuant to §§301-309 of the Illegal Immigration Reform and Immigrant Responsibility Act of 1996 (IIRIRA, P.L. 104-208, Div. C), deportation and exclusion proceedings were combined into a unified "removal" proceeding (INA §240); and immigration judges were given discretion to permit aliens who are subject to removal to "voluntarily depart" in lieu of facing formal removal proceedings (INA §240B).

[39] "Aliens" is synonymous with non-citizens, including legal permanent residents, temporary nonimmigrants, and unauthorized aliens.

[40] INA §212(a)(9).

[41] INA §276.

[42] Most non-Mexican aliens, however, were placed in formal removal proceedings and, after 2005, were normally detained until a removal order was implemented (see in this report "DHS Secure Border Initiative").

[43] Aliens who indicate an intention to apply for asylum or a fear of persecution are not subject to formal removal; for a fuller discussion of expedited removal see archived CRS Report RL33109, Immigration Policy on Expedited Removal of Aliens, by Alison Siskin and Ruth Ellen Wasem.

[44] Ibid. Under the 2006 policy, most Mexicans apprehended at the Southwest border were not placed in expedited removal proceedings unless they had previous criminal convictions.

[45] CBP's expanded use of reinstatement of removal depended, in part, on its ability to identify repeat offenders by enrolling their biometric data in the Automated Biometric Identification System (IDENT) system, a database of over 150 million individual records. For a fuller discussion of the US-VISIT system see CRS Report R43356, Border Security: Immigration Inspections at Ports of Entry, by Lisa Seghetti.

[46] Aliens apprehended at the border may face federal immigration-related criminal charges for illegal entry (8 U.S.C. §1325) or (on a second or subsequent apprehension) illegal re-entry (8 U.S.C. §1326), and in some cases they may face charges related to human smuggling (8 U.S.C. §1324) and visa and document fraud (18 U.S.C. §1546), among other charges. Unlawful presence in the United States absent additional factors, however, is a civil violation, not a criminal offense. See CRS Report RL32480, Immigration Consequences of Criminal Activity, by Michael John Garcia.

[47] A total of about 3,000 people were transferred to Mexico for prosecution under the program in FY2005-FY2012, according to data provided to CRS by CBP Office of Congressional Affairs.

[48] See U.S. Congress, House Committee on Homeland Security, Subcommittee on Border and Maritime Security, Does Administrative Amnesty Harm our Efforts to Gain and Maintain Operational Control of the Border, testimony of U.S. Border Patrol Chief Michael J. Fisher, 112th Cong., 1st sess., October 4, 2011.

[49] Ibid.

[50] See U.S. Congress, House Committee on Homeland Security, Subcommittee on Border and Maritime Security, Does Administrative Amnesty Harm our Efforts to Gain and Maintain Operational Control of the Border, testimony of U.S. Border Patrol Chief Michael J. Fisher, 112th Cong., 1st sess., October 4, 2011. Most alien smugglers reportedly charge aliens a set fee to enter the United States regardless of the number of attempts, so one goal of the high consequence enforcement programs is to disrupt smugglers' business model.

[51] Ibid. The Consequence Delivery System was formally launched January 1, 2011.

[52] Alan Bersin, The State of US/Mexico Border Security, Center for American Progress, August 4, 2011. Under section 240B of the Immigration and Nationality Act (INA), immigration officers and/or immigration judges may permit certain aliens to depart the United States in

lieu of (or at the termination of) a formal removal hearing, a process known as "voluntary departure" or "voluntary return." Bersin indicated that certain aliens may still be eligible for voluntary return, such as aliens younger than 18 years old traveling without a parent or legal guardian (i.e., unaccompanied minors).

[53] CRS attempted to obtain more current data (i.e., FY2013 and FY2014); however, according to DHS the data are not available for release. CRS email with DHS Congressional Affairs office on November 13, 2014.

[54] CRS attempted to obtain more current data (i.e., FY2013 and FY2014); however, according to DHS the data are not available for release. CRS email with DHS Congressional Affairs office on November 13, 2014.

[55] CRS attempted to obtain more current data (i.e., FY2013 and FY2014); however, according to DHS the data are not available for release. CRS email with DHS Congressional Affairs office on November 13, 2014.

[56] According to CBP Office of Congressional Affairs (April 24, 2013), aliens repatriated through the Alien Transfer Exit Program (ATEP) typically are voluntarily returned or subject to expedited removal. Thus, ATEP's high recidivism rates are partly a result of the relatively high rates associated with these two outcomes.

[57] This section was authored by Jerome Bjelopera, Specialist in Organized Crime and Terrorism.

[58] Memo from Jeh Charles Johnson, Secretary, Department of Homeland Security, to R. Gil Kerlikowske, Commissioner, U.S. Customs and Border Protection, et al., November 20, 2014.

[59] Ibid.

[60] Ibid.

[61] Ibid.

[62] Ibid.

[63] Ibid.

[64] See Figure 2 for sources. Due to the manner in which the Border Patrol collects and organizes its data, all statistics presented in this report (except where otherwise indicated) are based on the federal fiscal year, which begins October 1 and ends on September 30. All dollar amounts in this report are nominal values for the year from which data are reported.

[65] Account-level data are from the House Explanatory Statement to accompany P.L. 113-76. Also see CRS Report R43417, Forest Service Appropriations, FY2010-FY2014: In Brief, by Katie Hoover.

[66] Ibid.

[67] Department of Homeland Security, "Secure and Manage Our Borders," http:// www.dhs.gov/xabout/ gc_1240606351110.shtm.

[68] Over one-third of all federal criminal cases commenced in 2011-12 were for immigration cases; see U.S. Courts, U.S. District Courts - Criminal Cases Commenced, by Offense, Washington, DC, 2011, http://www.uscourts.gov/uscourts/ Statistics/JudicialBusiness/ 2012/appendices/D02DSep12.pdf. The prosecution of these cases involves expenditures by DOJ prosecutors, federal marshals, the federal bureau of prisons, and the U.S. district and magistrate court systems, among others. The costs of border enforcement borne by federal law enforcement and judicial officials outside of DHS are difficult to describe because these agencies do not list border-specific obligations in their budget documents. Also see National Research Council Committee on Estimating Costs of Immigration Enforcement in the Department of Justice, op. cit.

[69] The Immigration Act of 1990 (P.L. 101-649) authorized an increase of 1,000 Border Patrol agents; the IIRIRA (P.L. 104-208, Div. C) authorized an increase of a total of 5,000 Border

Patrol agents in FY1997-FY2001; the Uniting and Strengthening America by Providing Appropriate Tools Required to Intercept and Obstruct Terrorism Act (USA PATRIOT, P.L. 107-56) authorized INS to triple the number of Border Patrol agents at the northern border; and the Intelligence Reform and Terrorism Prevention Act (P.L. 108-458) authorized an increase of 10,000 Border Patrol agents between FY2006 and FY2010.

[70] U.S. Customs and Border Protection, Stats and Summaries, Border Patrol Agent Staffing by Fiscal Year, http://www.cbp.gov/sites/default/files/documents/BP%20Staffing%20FY1992-FY2014_0.pdf.

[71] See CRS Report R41286, Securing America's Borders: The Role of the Military, by R. Chuck Mason.

[72] P.L. 101-510. Div. A, Title X, §1004; also see Ibid.

[73] 32 U.S.C. §§502(a) and 502(f); also see CRS Report R41286, Securing America's Borders: The Role of the Military, by R. Chuck Mason.

[74] See CRS Report R41286, Securing America's Borders: The Role of the Military, by R. Chuck Mason.

[75] Ibid.

[76] Associated Press, "National Guard Troops at Mexico Border Cut to Fewer Than 300," USA Today, December 20, 2011.

[77] Homeland Security Today, "Pentagon Extends Deployment of National Guard in CBP Air Support Mission," December 7, 2012.

[78] Customs and Border Protection, "Tactical Infrastructure: History and Purpose," http://www.cbp.gov/xp/cgov/ border_security/ti/about_ti/ti_history.xml.

[79] P.L. 104-208, Div. C

[80] P.L. 109-367

[81] P.L. 109-367 subsequently identified five specific stretches of the border where fencing was to be installed; CBP Congressional Affairs provided CRS with this estimate of the total mileage covered by the law on September 25, 2006.

[82] P.L. 110-161, Div. E, §564. Unlike under prior law, the Consolidated Appropriations Act, as enacted, does not specify that reinforced fencing be "at least 2 layers." See P.L. 104-208, Div. C, §102(b), as amended by P.L. 109-367, §3.

[83] P.L. 110-161, Div. E, §564.

[84] Testimony of DHS Secretary Janet Napolitano before the Senate Judiciary Committee, The Border Security, Economic Opportunity, and Immigration Modernization Act, S. 744, 113th Cong., 1st sess., April 23, 2013.

[85] See, for example, testimony of DHS Inspector General Richard L. Skinner before the House Homeland Security Committee, Subcommittee on Management, Integration, and Oversight, New Secure Border Initiative, 109th Cong., 1st sess., December 16, 2005; GAO, Secure Border Initiative: DHS Needs to Address Significant Risks in Delivering Key Technology Investment, GAO-08-1086, September 22, 2008; and GAO, Secure Border Initiative: Technology Deployment Delays Persist and the Impact of Border Fencing Has Not Been Assessed, GAO-09-896, http://www.gao.gov/new.items/d09896.pdf.

[86] See DHS Inspector General (DHS IG), Secure Border Initiative: DHS Needs to Address Significant Risks in Delivering Key Technology Investment, DHS OIG-09-80, Washington, DC, June 2009; DHS IG, Controls Over SBInet Program Cost and Schedule Could Be Improved, DHS OIG-10-96, Washington, DC, June 2010.

[87] Testimony of CBP Assistant Commissioner Mark Borkowski before the House Committee on Homeland Security, Subcommittee on Border and Maritime Security, After SBInet–The Future of Technology on the Border, 112th Cong., 1st sess., March 15, 2011.

[88] DHS, Report on the Assessment of the Secure Border Initiative Network (SBInet) Program, Washington, DC, 2010, p. 1.

[89] 2012 data from U.S. Border Patrol Office of Congressional Affairs November 8, 2012; FY2006 data from DHS Congressional Budget Justification 2006; 2005 data from GAO, "Border Security: Key Unresolved Issues Justify Reevaluation of Border Surveillance Technology Program," GAO-06-295, February 2006.

According to a 2014 GAO report, in addition to the technology programs mentioned in the text, the plan also includes the following technologies: Integrated Fixes Towers, Agent Portable Surveillance System, and Thermal Imaging Devices. GAO Report to Congressional Requesters, "Arizona Border Surveillance Technology Plan: Additional Actions Needed to Strengthen Management and Assess Effectiveness," March 2014.

[90] U.S. Congress, Senate Committee on the Judiciary, The Future of Drones in America: Law Enforcement and Privacy Considerations, testimony of DHS Acting Officer for Civil Rights and Civil Liberties Tamara Kessler, 113th Congress, 1st sess., March 20, 2013.

[91] CBP Office of Congressional Affairs, March 19, 2013.

[92] Ibid.; and CBP Office of Air and Marine, 2011 Air and Marine Milestones and Achievements," http://www.cbp.gov/ xp/cgov/border_security/am/operations/2011_achiev.xml.

[93] Northern border UAS are based in Grand Forks, ND; Southwest border UAS are based in Sierra Vista, AZ (four systems) and Corpus Christi, TX (one system); and maritime UAS are based in Corpus Christi, TX (one system) and in Cape Canaveral, FL (two systems).

[94] Ibid.

[95] CBP Office of Congressional Affairs, March 21, 2013.

[96] Deportable aliens located refer to Border Patrol apprehensions and ICE administrative arrests. Prior to 1952, data refer to Border Patrol apprehensions.

[97] "Border Security in the 21st Century." The spike in apprehensions in FY2014 can be largely attributed to the unaccompanied alien children crisis.

[98] As mentioned elsewhere in this report, the recent increase in apprehensions in the Rio Grande Valley sector can largely be attributed to the UAC phenomenon.

[99] Biometric data of persons apprehended are recorded in the Automated Biometric Identification System (IDENT) system. When Border Patrol agents enter aliens' biometric data in the IDENT system, the data are automatically checked against DHS' "recidivist" database, which is used to track repeat entrants, and its "lookout" database, which is used to identify criminal aliens. US-VISIT workstations also are fully interoperable with the Federal Bureau of Investigation's (FBI) 10-print Integrated Automated Fingerprint Identification System (IAFIS), a biometric database that includes data on criminal records and the Department of Defense's (DOD) Automated Biometric Identification System (ABIS), which contains national security data.

[100] CRS attempted to obtain more current data (i.e., FY2013 and FY2014); however, according to DHS the data are not available for release. CRS email with DHS Congressional Affairs office on November 13, 2014.

[101] These calculations are based on aggregate data provided to CRS.

[102] For a fuller discussion, see U.S. Government Accountability Office (GAO), Border Patrol: Key Elements of Strategic Plan not Yet in Place to Inform Border Security Status and Resource Needs, GAO-13-25, December 2012 (hereafter: GAO, Key Elements of Strategic Plan). Also see Elliot Spagat, "Under Pressure, Border Patrol Now Counts Getaways," Associate Press, April 22, 2013.

[103] Ibid., p. 30.

[104] Mexicans accounted for about 59% of unauthorized migrants in the United States in 2011; see Michael Hoefer, Nancy Rytina, and Bryan Baker, Estimates of the Unauthorized Immigrant Population Residing in the United States: January 2011, Department of Homeland Security, Office of Immigration Statistics, Washington, DC, March 2011. For a fuller discussion, see CRS Report R42560, Mexican Migration to the United States: Policy and Trends, coordinated by Ruth Ellen Wasem.

[105] NRC, Options for Estimating Illegal Entries, pp. 5-4 – 5-15.

[106] See for example, Wayne A. Cornelius and Idean Salehyan, "Does border enforcement deter unauthorized immigration? The case of Mexican migration to the United States of America," Regulation & Governance 1.2 (2007): pp. 139-153; Manuela Angelucci, "U.S. Border Enforcement and the Net Flow of Mexican Illegal Migration," Economic Development and Cultural Change, 60, 2 (2012):311-357.

[107] CRS Calculations based on data provided by Princeton University Mexico Migration Project. All figures are based on three-year moving averages of annual apprehension probabilities.

[108] CRS calculations based on data provided by University of California-San Diego Mexico Migration Field Research Project. All figures are based on three-year moving averages of annual apprehension probabilities. Figures are based on total apprehensions divide by total trips, not once-or-more apprehension rates by individual migrants.

[109] Estimates provided by CBP Office of Congressional Affairs, April 24, 2013. Border Patrol reportedly estimates apprehensions using a methodology broadly similar to the capture-recapture method discussed elsewhere in this report (see "Estimating Illegal Flows Using Recidivism Data").

[110] Survey data on at-the-border deterrence may under-estimate deterrence rates due to the difficulty of measuring successful entry on a single trip, versus successful entry over the course of a lifetime.

[111] See Princeton University Mexican Migration Project, "Access to Border-Crossing Guides and Family/Friends on First Undocumented Trip," http://mmp.opr.princeton.edu/ results/ 002coyote-en.aspx.

[112] See Bryan Roberts, Gordon Hanson, and Derekh Cornwell et al., An Analysis of Migrant Smugglng Costs along the Southwest Border, DHS Office of Immigration Statistics, Washington, DC, November 2010. The extent to which smugglers may pass their costs along to migrants also depends on the elasticity of migration with respect to such costs, as Roberts et al. discuss; smuggling fees may also therefore depend on the broader migration context, including economic "pulls" and "pushes" in the United States and its migration partner states.

[113] All data are CRS calculations based on data provided by Princeton University Mexico Migration Project and UCSD Mexican Migration Field Research Project.

[114] See for example, U.S. Congress, House Committee on Homeland Security, Subcommittee on Borders and Maritime Security, Measuring Outcomes to Understand the State of Border Security, 113th Congress, 1st sess., March 20, 2013; U.S. Congress, Senate Committee on Homeland Security and Governmental Affairs, Border Security: Measuring Progress and Addressing the Challenges, 113th Congress, 1st sess., March 14, 2013.

[115] U.S. Congress, House Committee on Homeland Security, Subcommittee on Borders and Maritime Security, Measuring Outcomes to Understand the State of Border Security, testimony of Assistant Commissioner of Homeland Security Mark Borkowski, 113th Congress, 1st sess., March 20, 2013; U.S. Congress, House Committee on Homeland Security, Subcommittee on Borders and Maritime Security, Measuring Outcomes to Understand the State of Border Security, testimony of Border Patrol Chief Michael Fisher,

113th Congress, 1st sess., March 20, 2013. Also see U.S. Congress, House Committee on Homeland Security, Subcommittee on Border and Maritime Security, What Does a Secure Border Look Like, testimony by Marc R. Rosenblum, 113th Cong., 1st sess., February 26, 2013.

[116] See Edward Alden and Bryan Roberts, "Are U.S. Borders Secure? Why We Don't Know and How to Find Out," Foreign Affairs 90, 4 (2011): pp. 19-26.

[117] For a fuller discussion, see GAO, Key Elements of Strategic Plan, pp. 28-31.

[118] See for example, Andrew Becker, "New Drone Radar Reveals Border Patrol 'Gotaways' in High Numbers," Center for Investigative Reporting, April 4, 2013.

[119] GAO, Key Elements of Strategic Plan, p. 24.

[120] For a fuller discussion of border metric methodologies and additional estimates of border security, also see Bryan Roberts, John Whitley and Edward Alden, Managing Illegal Immigration to the United States: How Effective is Enforcement? New York: Council on Foreign Relations Press, 2013 (hereafter: Roberts et al., Managing Illegal Immigration to the United States).

[121] For a clear discussion of this methodology, see Jeffrey S. Passel, "The Size and Characteristics of the Unauthorized Migrant Population in the U.S.," Pew Hispanic Center, March 6, 2006, http://www.pewhispanic.org/2006/03/07/sizeand-characteristics-of-the-unauthorized-migrant-population-in-the-us/. Also see CRS Report RL33874, Unauthorized Aliens Residing in the United States: Estimates Since 1986, by Ruth Ellen Wasem.

[122] In general, unauthorized migrants enter the United States three ways: by crossing the border without inspection between ports of entry (the focus of this report); by entering illegally through ports of entry, either by using a fraudulent document or by hiding in a vehicle; or by entering legally and then overstaying a temporary visa or becoming deportable for some other reason.

[123] See Department of Justice, FY2001 Performance Report & FY2002 Revised Final, FY2003 Performance Plan, Washington, DC 2001, pp. 120-122.

[124] See, for example, Edward Alden and Bryan Roberts, "Are US Borders Secure? Why We Don't Know, and How to Find Out," Foreign Affairs, vol. 90, no. 4 (July/August 2011), pp. 19-26.

[125] U.S. Government Accountability Office, Border Security: Preliminary Observations on Border Control Measuers for the Southwest Border, GAO-11-374T, February 15, 2011, p. 7.

[126] Ibid., p. 8.

[127] U.S. Congress, House Committee on Homeland Security, Subcommittee on Border and Maritime Security, Securing Our Borders: Operational Control and the Path Forward, 112th Congress, 1st sess., February 15, 2010.

[128] DHS did not report on border miles under effective control in its FY2010 Annual Performance Report; see DHS, Annual Performance Report: Fiscal Years 2010-2012, Washington, DC, April 2011, http://www.dhs.gov/xlibrary/ assets/cfo_apr_fy2010.pdf.

[129] CBP Office of Congressional Affairs, March 15, 2013.

[130] U.S. Congress, House Committee on Homeland Security, Subcommittee on Borders and Maritime Security, Measuring Outcomes to Understand the State of Border Security, testimony of Border Patrol Chief Michael Fisher, 113th Congress, 1st sess., March 20, 2013.

[131] U.S. Congress, Senate Committee on Homeland Security and Governmental Affairs, Securing the Border: Progress at the Federal Level, testimony of Secretary of Homeland Security Janet Napolitano, 112th Cong., 1st sess., May 4, 2011.

[132] CBP Office of Congressional Affairs, December 9, 2011.

[133] U.S. Congress, House Committee on Homeland Security, Subcommittee on Borders and Maritime Security, Measuring Outcomes to Understand the State of Border Security, testimony of Assistant Commissioner of Homeland Security Mark Borkowski, 113th Congress, 1st sess., March 20, 2013.

[134] Ibid.

[135] That is, whereas using apprehensions as a metric of border security is problematic because apprehensions depend on border resources, the ratio of apprehensions to got aways is somewhat less problematic because both apprehensions and estimated known got aways depend on resources, so the ratio may more accurately reflect the proportion of aliens that successfully enters. Nonetheless, the ratio may still be sensitive to border resources if estimating inflows is less (or more) resource-intensive than apprehending aliens. And the enforcement rate by itself may not be an acceptable metric without also considering data on total illegal attempts: many would consider a 10% effectiveness rate based on 100 entry attempts to be more effective than a 90% rate based on a million attempts, for example.

[136] According to CBP Office of Congressional Affairs December 20, 2011 and more recent CRS conversations with DHS officials, DHS reportedly plans to use a capture-recapture model as one element of the border conditions index (BCI).

[137] Thomas J. Espenshade, "Using INS Border Apprehension Data to Measure the Flow of Undocumented Migrants Crossing the U.S.-Mexico Frontier," International Migration Review, vol. 29, no. 2 (Summer 1995), pp. 545-565.

[138] In statistical methods, the odds of apprehension equal the probability of apprehension divided by one minus the probability of apprehension; see Ibid.

[139] Ibid. The basic model also assumes that that the odds of being apprehended are the same across different border regions and across multiple attempts to cross the border.

[140] Mexicans accounted for 87% of USBP apprehensions in FY2010, 84% in FY2011, and 73% in FY2012, the three lowest proportions ever recorded.

[141] See Roberts et al., Managing Illegal Immigration to the United States); Panel on Survey Options for Estimating the Flow of Unauthorized Crossings at the U.S.-Mexico Border, Options for Estimating Illegal Entries at the U.S.-Mexico Border, Washington, DC: National Research Council, 2012 (hereafter: NRC, Options for Estimating Illegal Entries). Accounting for deterrence, flows are estimated to be equal to the number of total apprehensions divided by the the odds of successful enforcement; and the probability of successful enforcement is defined as the number of recidivists divided by total apprehensions, divided by one minus the probability of deterrence.

[142] Princeton University Mexican Migration Project, "Probability of a Mexican Taking a First U.S. Trip," http://mmp.opr.princeton.edu/results/009firsttrip-en.aspx.

[143] Jeffrey Passel and D'Vera Cohn, "Unauthorized Immigrants: 11.1 Million in 2011," Pew Hispanic Center, December 6, 2012, http://www.pewhispanic.org/2012/12/06/unauthorized-immigrants-11-1-million-in-2011/; also see CRS Report R42988, U.S. Immigration Policy: Chart Book of Key Trends, by William A. Kandel.

[144] Jeffrey Passel, D'Vera Cohn and Ana Gonzalez-Barrera, "Net Migration from Mexico Falls to Zero—and Perhaps Less," Washington, DC: Pew Hispanic Center, May 3, 2012.

[145] GAO, Key Elements of Strategic Plan, pp. 74-82. Effectiveness rates in this paragraph are defined as the proportion of known illegal entrants who are apprehended or return to Mexico; effectiveness rates are lower if turn-backs are not counted in the numerator.

[146] As Figure 9 illustrates, the model estimates that illegal inflows reached their lowest point in 2009 if deterrence is assumed to be 40%, while inflows reached their lowest point in 2011 if deterrence is assumed to be 20%.

[147] See, for example, Douglas S. Massey, Joaquin Arango, and Graeme Hugo et al., Worlds In Motion: Understanding International Migration at the End of the Millenium, 2nd ed. (New York: Oxford University Press, 2005).

[148] On the effects of Mexico's falling birthrate on U.S. immigration, see Gordon H. Hanson, Esther Duflo, and Craig McIntosh, "The Demography of Mexican Migration to the United States," American Economic Review, vol. 99, no. 2 (May 2009), pp. 22-27. Also see CRS Report R42560, Mexican Migration to the United States: Policy and Trends, coordinated by Ruth Ellen Wasem.

[149] Among Mexicans who migrated illegally to look for work (83% of those in the survey), 60% of those repatriated in 2010 reported that they intended to return to the United States immediately, and 80% reported that they intended to return eventually, down from 81% and 92%, respectively, in 2005. Among new unauthorized migrants (those who had spent less than a week in the United States before being repatriated to Mexico), 18% of those repatriated in 2010 reported that they would not return to the United States compared to 6% in 2005. See Jeffrey Passel, D'Vera Cohn, and Ana Gonzalez-Barrera, Net Migration from Mexico Falls to Zero—And Perhaps Less, Pew Hispanic Center, Washington, DC, 2012, http://www.pewhispanic.org/files/2012/04/PHC-04-23a-Mexican-Migration.pdf, pp. 24-25.

[150] See for example, Scott Borger, Gordon Hanson, and Bryan Roberts "The Decision to Emigrate From Mexico," presentation at the Society of Government Economists annual conference, November 6, 2012; Manuela Angelucci, "U.S. Border Enforcement and the Net Flow of Mexican Illegal Migration," Economic Development and Cultural Change, 60, 2 (2012):311-357; Rebecca Lessem. "Mexico-US Immigration: Effects of Wages and Border Enforcement," Carnegie Mellon University, Research Showcase, May 2, 2012.

[151] See for example, Wayne Cornelius, "Evaluating Recent US Immigration Control Policy: What Mexican Migrants Can Tell Us," in Crossing and Controlling Borders: Immigration Policies and Their Impact on Migrants' Journeys, ed. Mechthild Baumann, Astrid Lorenz, and Kerstin Rosenhow (Farmington, MI: Budrich Unipress Ltd, 2011); Douglas S. Massey, Jorge Durand, and Nolan J. Malone, Beyond Smoke and Mirrors: Mexican Immigration in an Era of Economic Integration (Russell Sage Foundation, 2002).

[152] See Manuela Angelucci, "U.S. Border Enforcement and the Net Flow of Mexican Illegal Migration," Economic Development and Cultural Change, 60, 2 (2012):311-357.

[153] See CRS Report R42057, Interior Immigration Enforcement: Programs Targeting Criminal Aliens, by Marc R. Rosenblum and William A. Kandel.

[154] In 2011, for example, of the 238 migrants deaths for which DHS was able to determine a cause of death, 139 were attributed to exposure to heat or cold or water-related; data provided to CRS by CBP Office of Congressional Affairs December 15, 2011.

[155] Also see Karl Eschbach, Jacqueline Hagan, and Nestor Rodriguez et al., "Death at the Border," International Migration Review, vol. 33, no. 2 (Summer 1999), pp. 430-454.

[156] National Strategic Plan, p. 11-12.

[157] The USBP's Border Patrol Search, Trauma, and Rescue Unit (BORSTAR) is comprised of agents with specialized skills and training for tactical medical search and rescue operations. BORSTAR agents provide rapid response to search and rescue and medical operations, including rescuing migrants in distress.

[158] For a fuller discussion, see CRS Report R41075, Southwest Border Violence: Issues in Identifying and Measuring Spillover Violence, by Kristin Finklea.

[159] See for example, Daniel Borunda, "El Paso Ranked Safest Large city in U.S. for 3rd Straight Year," El Paso Times, February 6, 2013, http://www.elpasotimes.com/ci_22523903/el-paso-ranked-safest-large-city-u-s.

[160] Uniform Crime Report (UCR) data provide the most information about crime rates, but they are not sufficiently fine-tuned to provide information on the diverse factors affecting such trends; see CRS Report RL34309, How Crime in the United States Is Measured, by Nathan James and Logan Rishard Council.

[161] See Stanley Bailey, Karl Eschbach, and Jacqueline Hagan et al., "Migrant Death on the US-Mexco Border 1985- 1996," University of Houston Center for Immigration Research Working Paper Series, vol. 96, no. 1 (1996); Jimenez, "Humanitarian Crisis," 2009.

[162] The Border Patrol has drawn criticism from human rights activists who claim that the agency's migrant death count understates the number of fatalities. Some contend that the Border Patrol undercounts fatalities by excluding skeletal remains, victims in car accidents, and corpses discovered by other agencies or local law enforcement officers; see, for example, Raymond Michalowski, "Border Militarization and Migrant Suffering: A Case of Transnational Social Injury," Social Justice, Summer 2007.

[163] Also see Adam Isacson and Maureen Meyer, "Border Security and Migration: A Report from South Texas," Washington Office on Latin America, http://www.wola.org/sites/default/files/downloadable/Mexico/2013/Border%20Security%20and%20Migration%20South%20Texas.pdf.

[164] See Wayne Cornelius, "Evaluating Recent US Immigration Control Policy: What Mexican Migrants Can Tell Us," in Crossing and Controlling Borders: Immigration Policies and Their Impact on Migrants' Journeys, ed. Mechthild Baumann, Astrid Lorenz, and Kerstin Rosenhow (Farmington, MI: Budrich Unipress Ltd, 2011); Douglas S. Massey, Jorge Durand, and Nolan J. Malone, Beyond Smoke and Mirrors: Mexican Immigration in an Era of Economic Integration (Russell Sage Foundation, 2002).

[165] Whereas almost half of unauthorized aliens from Mexico who arrived in 1980 remained in the United States for less than a year, fewer than 20% of unauthorized Mexicans who entered in 2010 returned home within a year; see Mexican Migration Project, "Probability of Return within 12 Months," http://mmp.opr.princeton.edu/results/010returnpersen.aspx. Also see Jonathan Hicken, Mollie Cohen, and Jorge Narvaez, "Double Jeopardy: How U.S. Enforcement Policies Shape Tunkaseño Migration," in Mexican Migration and the U.S. Economic Crisis, ed. Wayne A. Cornelius, David FitzGerald, Pedro Lewin Fischer, and Leah Muse-Orlinoff (La Jolla, CA: University of California, San Diego Center for Comparative Immigration Studies, 2010), pp. 56-57. And whereas an estimated 60-90% of unauthorized migrants during the 1970s were single men, by 2008 men only accounted for an estimated 53% of unauthorized aliens, with women representing 34% and the remainder children; see Jeffrey S. Passel and D'Vera Cohn, A Portrait of Unauthorized Immigrants in the United States, Pew Hispanic Center, Washington, DC, April 14, 2009, p. 4, http://pewhispanic.org/files/reports/107.pdf.

[166] For example, changes in U.S. labor markets have resulted in more permanent (non-seasonal) employment opportunities for unauthorized aliens as well as more employment opportunities for unauthorized women; See CRS Report R41592, The U.S. Foreign-Born Population: Trends and Selected Characteristics, by William A. Kandel.

[167] Half of the Mexico-based family members of unauthorized aliens interviewed by the UC, San Diego MMFRP in 2009 indicated that they had a relative who had remained in the United States longer than they had intended because they feared they would be unable to reenter the United States if they returned home; see Hicken et al. "Double Jeopardy," 57-58.

[168] Hicken et al., "Double Jeopardy," pp. 60-61.

[169] Probability of apprehension on an alien's most recent attempt to illegally pass through a port of entry was 0.36, compared to 0.73 on the most recent entry attempt between ports of entry; UC San Diego MMFRP data provided to CRS September 23, 2010.

[170] CBP Office of Congressional Affairs March 21, 2013.

[171] See for example, Adolfo Flores and Ruben Vives, "New Panga Incident Investigated as Possible Smuggling Operation," Los Angeles Times, December 10, 2012; Dave Graham, "By Land or by Sea, Tougher U.S. Border Tests Illegal Immigrants," Reuters, March 20, 2013. Border tunnels are mainly used to smuggle narcotics into the United States, rather than for illegal migration.

[172] Department of Homeland Security, Environmental Impact Statement for the Completion of the 14-mile Border Infrastructure System, San Diego, California (July 2003), pp. 1-11.

[173] According to the GAO, about 25% of the northern border and 43% of the Southwest border consist of federal and tribal lands overseen by the U.S. Forest Service and Department of the Interior; see CRS Report R42346, Federal Land Ownership: Overview and Data, by Carol Hardy Vincent, Laura A. Hanson, and Jerome P. Bjelopera.

[174] See for example, University of Texas School of Law, "The Texas-Mexico Border Wall," http://www.utexas.edu/ law/centers/humanrights/borderwall/.

[175] See CRS Report R42053, Fiscal Impacts of the Foreign-Born Population, by William A. Kandel. Although the overall economic effects of migration—and unauthorized migration in particular—are difficult to estimate, research suggests that fiscal costs of migration are disproportionately borne at the local level.

[176] See, for example, Mark Harrison, "Beefed Up Border Patrol Jolts Farmers, Cows," Seattle Times, November 13, 2011; Rafael Carranza, "Leaders Blame Lost Business Deals on Border Fence," KGBT Channel 4 News, November 2, 2009, http://www.valleycentral.com/news/story.aspx?id=371266#.Tt0oAmNM8rs.

[177] See, for example, Associated Press, "Quebec-Vermont Border Communities Divided by Post-9/11 Security," CBC News: Canada, August 14, 2011.

[178] See, for example, NY School of Law, NY Civil Liberties Union, and Families for Freedom, Justice Derailed: What Raids On New York's Trains And Buses Reveal About Border Patrol's Interior Enforcement Practices, New York: November, 2011, http://www.nyclu.org/publications/report-justice-derailed-what-raids-trains-and-buses-reveal-aboutborder-patrols-interi; Lornet Turnbull and Roberto Daza, "Climate of Fear Grips Forks Illegal Immigrants," Seattle Times, June 26, 2011.

[179] See for example, American Civil Liberties Union, "Immigration Reform Should Eliminate Operation Streamline," http://www.aclu.org/files/assets/operation_streamline_issue_ brief.pdf.

[180] See for example, Alan Gomez, "Lawsuits Allege abuses by Border Patrol Agents," USA Today, March 13, 2013; Judith Greene and Alexis Mazón, "Privately Operated Federal Prisons for Immigrants: Expensive, Unsafe, Unenecessary," Justice Strategies, September 13, 2012; No More Deaths/No Mas Muertes, A Culture of Cruelty: Abuse and Impunity in Short-Term U.S. Border Patrol Custody, 2011.

[181] See, for example, National Immigration Forum, Operation Streamline: Unproven Benefits Outweighed by Costs to Taxpayers, Washington, DC, September 2012.

[182] Thomas H. Cohen, Special Report: Pretrial Detention and Misconduct in Federal District Courts, 1995-2010, U.S. Department of Justice, Bureau of Justice Statistics, NCJ 239673, Washington, DC, February 2013.

[183] Mark Motivans, Immigration Offenders in the Federal Justice System, 2010, U.S. Department of Justice, Bureau of Justice Statistics, NCJ 238581, Washington, DC, July 2012.

[184] Administrative Office of the U.S. Courts, Report on the Impact on the Judiciary of Law Enforcement Activities Along the Southwest Border, Washington, DC: Administrative Office of the U.S. Courts, July 2008.

[185] DHS, "Beyond the Border Action Plan," December 2011, http://www.dhs.gov/files/publications/beyond-the-borderaction-plan.shtm; also see CRS Report 96-397, Canada-U.S. Relations, coordinated by Ian F. Fergusson and Derek E. Mix.

[186] See for example, Dana Gabriel, "Toward a North American Police State and Security Perimeter: U.S.-Canada 'Beyond the Border Agreement,'" Global Research, May 14, 2012.

[187] See CRS Report R41349, U.S.-Mexican Security Cooperation: The Mérida Initiative and Beyond, by Clare Ribando Seelke and Kristin Finklea.

[188] See CRS Report R42560, Mexican Migration to the United States: Policy and Trends, coordinated by Ruth Ellen Wasem; Marc R. Rosenblum, Obstacles and Opportunities for Regional Cooperation: The US-Mexico Case, Migration Policy Institute, April 2011, http://www.migrationpolicy.org/pubs/USMexico-cooperation.pdf.

[189] Thomas J. Espenshade, "Using INS Border Apprehension Data to Measure the Flow of Undocumented Migrants Crossing the U.S.-Mexico Frontier," International Migration Review, vol. 29, no. 2 (Summer 1995), pp. 545-565.

[190] Ibid., pp. 549-550.

[191] CRS analysis of apprehensions data from DHS, Yearbook of Immigration Statistics FY2011, Washington, DC: DHS, 2012. Mexicans accounted for 90% of all apprehensions in 2000-2009, before falling to 83% in 2010 and 76% in FY2011 (Mexicans represent a lower proportion of all apprehensions than of Border Patrol apprehensions; total apprehensions data for FY2012 were not available when this report was released).

[192] Espenshade, "Using INS Border Apprehension Data," pp. 551-552.

[193] Ibid., p. 554.

[194] The Consequence Delivery System seeks to reduce recidivism by increasing the proportion of aliens subject to formal removal, criminal charges, and/or remote repatriation (see "CBP Consequence Delivery System"). And unauthorized aliens from countries other than Mexico (i.e., 73% of USBP apprehensions in FY2012) typically are deported to their home countries, substantially raising the cost of re-entry.

[195] Roberts et al., Managing Illegal Immigration to the United States.

[196] CBP Office of Congressional Affairs, December 20, 2011.

[197] DHS also reportedly restricts its recidivism analysis to Mexican aliens, but may uses country-specific recidivism data to calculate apprehension rates, and may therefore estimate a somewhat lower probability of successful enforcement based on this methodology.

In: Barriers and Migration Control
Editor: Arthur Rivera

ISBN: 978-1-63483-308-0

Chapter 2

BARRIERS ALONG THE U.S. BORDERS: KEY AUTHORITIES AND REQUIREMENTS*

Michael John Garcia

SUMMARY

Securing the borders is an issue of perennial concern to Congress. Federal law authorizes the Department of Homeland Security (DHS) to construct barriers along the U.S. borders to deter illegal crossings. DHS is also required to construct reinforced fencing along at least 700 miles of the land border with Mexico (a border that stretches 1,933 miles), though Congress has not provided a deadline for its completion. At this time, fence construction has largely been halted, though DHS still needs to deploy fencing along nearly 50 additional miles of the southwest border to satisfy the 700-mile requirement.

The primary statute authorizing DHS to deploy barriers along the international borders is Section 102 of the Illegal Immigration Reform and Immigrant Responsibility Act of 1996 (IIRIRA; P.L. 104-208, div. C). Congress made significant amendments to IIRIRA Section 102 through three enactments—the REAL ID Act of 2005 (P.L. 109-13, div. B), the Secure Fence Act of 2006 (P.L. 109-367), and the Consolidated Appropriations Act, 2008 (P.L. 110-161, div. E). These amendments required that DHS construct hundreds of miles of new fencing along the

---

* This is an edited, reformatted and augmented version of a Congressional Research Service publication R43975, prepared for Members and Committees of Congress, dated April 8, 2015.

border, and also provided the Secretary of DHS with broad authority to waive "all legal requirements" that may impede construction of barriers and roads under IIRIRA Section 102. These statutory modifications, along with increased funding for border projects, resulted in the deployment of several hundred miles of new barriers along the southwest border between 2005 and 2011. In recent years, DHS has largely stopped deploying additional fencing along the border, as the agency has altered its enforcement strategy in a manner that places less priority upon fencing.

As amended by the Secure Fence Act in 2006, IIRIRA Section 102(b) required DHS to install at least two layers of reinforced fencing along five stretches of the southwest border totaling more than 700 miles. IIRIRA was substantially revised just over a year later by the Consolidated Appropriations Act, 2008, to replace this requirement with a mandate that DHS install reinforced fencing (but not necessarily in two or more layers) "along not less than 700 miles" of the border.

Section 102(b) provides that "notwithstanding" this requirement, DHS is not legally obligated to install fencing at "any particular location." One way to construe this clause is simply to indicate that, while DHS is required to install fencing along at least 700 miles of the border, it is not required to install any portion of the mandated fencing at any specific location (in contrast to the earlier requirement of the Secure Fence Act). An alternative interpretation of this clause has also been suggested (including by some DHS officials, but not consistently), under which DHS could potentially construct fencing along *less than 700 miles* of the border and satisfy the statute's fencing requirements, if it determined additional fencing to be unwarranted. This broad interpretation of the clause seems problematic, however, as it would render Section 102(b)'s provision requiring fencing "along not less than 700 miles" of the border meaningless. The legislative history behind the changes made to IIRIRA Section 102(b) also favors the narrower interpretation. Legislation in the 114th Congress, including H.R. 399, the Secure Our Borders First Act of 2015, as reported by the House Homeland Security Committee, would effectively mandate the completion of the remaining mileage and also provide additional fencing specifications.

This report discusses key statutory authorities and requirements governing DHS's construction of barriers along the U.S. borders. It also includes appendixes listing federal laws that have been waived by DHS in furtherance of border construction projects.

Securing the international borders of the United States has been an issue of perennial interest and importance to Congress. Federal law authorizes the Department of Homeland Security (DHS) to construct barriers along the U.S. borders to deter illegal crossings.[1] DHS is also required to construct reinforced fencing along at least 700 miles of the land border with Mexico,[2] though fencing is not required to be deployed at any "particular location" along that border.[3] Responsibility for carrying out these functions, and more generally securing the U.S. land borders between ports of entry, primarily falls to U.S. Border Patrol within DHS's Customs and Border Protection (CBP).[4]

The primary statute authorizing DHS to deploy barriers along the international borders is Section 102 of the Illegal Immigration Reform and Immigrant Responsibility Act of 1996 (IIRIRA).[5] Congress made significant amendments to IIRIRA Section 102 through three enactments—the REAL ID Act of 2005, the Secure Fence Act of 2006, and the Consolidated Appropriations Act, 2008.[6] These amendments established a mandate upon DHS to construct hundreds of miles of new fencing along the border, and also provided the Secretary of DHS with broad authority to waive "all legal requirements" that may impede construction of barriers and roads under IIRIRA Section 102.

These statutory modifications, along with increased funding for border projects, resulted in the deployment of several hundred miles of fencing and other barriers along the southwest land border between 2005 and 2011.[7] A portion of this infrastructure is fencing that is primarily intended to prevent illegal border crossings by foot (referred to by DHS as "pedestrian fencing"), while other types of barriers have been installed to impede vehicles from smuggling persons or contraband into the United States (referred to by DHS as "vehicle fencing"),[8] but which do not stop crossings by persons traveling on foot. In some instances, an additional layer of fencing (secondary fencing) may also be installed behind primary pedestrian fencing to further impede illegal crossings.

The efficacy of deploying additional fencing along the border has been the subject of debate among many policymakers, particularly regarding the cost, environmental impact, and effectiveness of border fencing in comparison to alternative means of deterring illegal crossings.[9] Largely on account of changes in DHS's border enforcement strategy and prioritization of resources,[10] the construction of additional fencing along the land border with Mexico has largely halted. In October 2014, DHS indicated that it had constructed a total of 352.7 miles of pedestrian fence (in addition 36.3 miles of secondary fencing), and 299 miles of vehicle fencing along the southwest border.[11] The total amount of pedestrian and vehicle fencing identified by DHS was slightly less than the 653 miles that U.S. Border Patrol had reportedly identified as appropriate for fencing and other barriers.[12] However, it appears that further fencing would need to be deployed in order for DHS to satisfy the statutory requirement that the agency construct fencing "along not less than 700 miles of the southwest border."[13]

IIRIRA Section 102(b), as most recently amended by the Consolidated Appropriations Act, 2008, provides that "notwithstanding" the requirement to deploy fencing along 700 miles of the southwest border, DHS is not obligated to install fencing at "any particular location." One way to construe this proviso is simply to indicate that, while DHS is required to install fencing along at least 700 miles of the border, it is not required to install any portion of the mandated fencing at any specific location (in contrast to the earlier requirement of the Secure Fence Act). An alternative interpretation of this proviso has also been suggested (including by some DHS officials, but not consistently), under which DHS could potentially construct fencing along *less than 700 miles* of the border and satisfy the statute's fencing requirements, if it determined additional fencing to be unwarranted. This broad interpretation of the proviso seems problematic, however, as it would render Section 102(b)'s provision requiring fencing "along not less than 700 miles" of the border meaningless. The legislative history behind the changes made to IIRIRA Section 102(b), along with the interpretation given to this provision by federal courts (albeit primarily in non-binding dicta), also favors the narrower interpretation.

Congress has not squarely addressed the appropriate interpretation of the fencing requirement in the following years. Members and congressional committees have arguably taken differing views regarding the nature of the fencing requirements in the years since the enactment of the most recent amendments to IIRIRA Section 102.[14]

Regardless of the appropriate interpretation of IIRIRA's requirement that DHS install fencing along 700 miles of the southwest border, the statute imposes no clear deadline for when DHS must deploy any contemplated fencing. In 2011, a legal challenge brought by the State of Arizona to compel completion of the fence along 700 miles of the border was dismissed by the reviewing federal district court, on the ground that the Arizona's challenge concerned activities which were committed to agency discretion and not subject to judicial review.[15]

In recent years, legislation has perennially been introduced to modify the statutory authorities governing DHS's deployment of fencing and other infrastructure along or near the border.[16] In the 113th Congress, the Senate-passed immigration reform bill, S. 744, would have required DHS to develop and implement a border security strategy, which would have included the construction of at least 700 miles of pedestrian fencing along the Southwest land border. Benchmarks for the implementation of these strategies would have constituted "triggers" to be achieved before many unlawfully present aliens would be permitted to first obtain provisional legal status, and then become eligible for full-fledged legal immigrant status. For its part in the 113th Congress, the House passed legislation, H.R. 5230, intended to facilitate CBP's border security activities on federal lands within 100 miles of the international borders, including by exempting application of specific laws to CBP border construction projects on such lands.

Legislation has also been introduced in the 114th Congress that would establish new fencing requirements along the southwest border or facilitate border construction projects on federal lands, including H.R. 399, as reported out of the House Committee on Homeland Security. Among other things, H.R. 399 would effectively require fencing along 700 miles of the border to be completed within 18 months, and would also specify the specific areas along the border where such fencing would be installed.[17]

This report provides an overview of the key statutory authorities and requirements governing DHS's construction of barriers along the international borders of the United States. It also includes appendixes listing federal laws that have been waived by DHS in furtherance of border construction projects.

KEY STATUTORY AUTHORITIES AND REQUIREMENTS

Prior to 1996, federal immigration statutes did not expressly authorize or require the construction of barriers along the U.S. international borders.[18] In the preceding years, authority to deploy any such barriers appears to have primarily derived from the general statutory responsibility of the Attorney General (and now the Secretary of Homeland Security)[19] to "guard the boundaries and borders of the United States against the illegal entry of aliens."[20] Perhaps the most prominent example of this general authority being employed to construct barriers occurred in the early 1990s, when the U.S. Border Patrol (with the assistance of the Department of Defense's Army Corps of Engineers) installed 10-foot-high, welded-steel fencing along roughly 14 miles of the border near San Diego.[21]

In 1996, Congress passed IIRIRA, which expressly instructed immigration authorities to construct barriers along the international land borders to deter unauthorized migration.[22] This requirement, contained in IIRIRA Section 102, has been amended on three occasions, and its current language can be viewed at *Appendix A*. Among other things, IIRIRA Section 102 in its current form:

- generally authorizes DHS to construct barriers and roads along the international borders, in order to deter illegal crossings at locations of high illegal entry;
- requires the construction of reinforced fencing covering at least 700 miles along the southwest border, though the Secretary is not required to install fencing at any particular location;
- requires a specified amount of fencing in priority areas along the southwest border, which DHS was instructed to have been completed by December 31, 2008; and
- provides the Secretary of DHS with authority to waive any legal requirements which may impede construction of barriers and roads under Section 102.[23]

The following sections discuss each of these requirements, including how they have been modified over the years.

General Authority to Install Barriers and Roads to Deter Illegal Crossings

Section 102(a) of IIRIRA provides that the Secretary of Homeland Security "shall take such actions as may be necessary to install additional physical barriers and roads ... in the vicinity of the United States border to deter illegal crossings in areas of high illegal entry into the United States." Although this provision is fashioned as a statutory command, providing that the Secretary "shall" take action,[24] this command is qualified by the language that follows, which affords the Secretary the discretion to determine the appropriate amount of "additional" barriers to deploy, as well as the most appropriate locations to install such barriers "to deter illegal crossings."[25]

To the extent that IIRIRA Section 102(a) constitutes a discrete, judicially reviewable command for the Secretary to construct "additional" fencing,[26] immigration authorities seem to have satisfied this mandate by deploying hundreds of miles of additional barriers and roads along the border since IIRIRA was enacted in 1996. Accordingly, this provision perhaps most reasonably could be construed as conferring general authority to the Secretary of Homeland Security to construct barriers and roads along the international borders, so as to deter crossings in areas of "high illegal entry" (a term not defined by the statute).[27] As discussed later in this report, more specific requirements are imposed upon the Secretary by IIRIRA Section 102(b), which requires the Secretary, in exercising the authority conferred under Section 102(a), to ensure that fencing and other barriers be deployed along specified mileage of the southwest border.[28]

Section 102(a) generally authorizes the construction of roads and physical barriers, without specifying any particular form that such barriers may take (e.g., reinforced fencing, multilayered fencing, or concrete barriers). Barriers and roads are authorized to be installed along any of the international borders of the United States, at least so long as the DHS determines their installation appropriate to deter unauthorized crossings in areas of high illegal entry.

The provision's authorization for the installation of barriers and roads applies to areas "in the vicinity of the United States border." The phrase "vicinity of the United States border" is not defined under IIRIRA, nor is it described in other federal immigration statutes. As a result, there may be some ambiguity as to the authorized distance from the border where roads and barriers may be constructed. The sole federal court to consider the usage of the term "vicinity" in IIRIRA Section 102 interpreted the term as including land "situated near the border," rather than only land directly adjacent to the border.[29]

Some DHS regulations unrelated to the border fence have described distances up to 25 miles from a location as being within its "vicinity."[30] The Supreme Court, in non-binding dicta, also once characterized a search occurring 25 miles from the border as being within the "general vicinity of the border,"[31] though it does not appear that the Court ascribed legal significance to that phrase. There is also no indication in the legislative history of IIRIRA, however, that Congress contemplated the term "vicinity of the United States border" as referring to a specific distance.[32]

Requirement for Installation of Fencing Along the Southwest Border

IIRIRA Section 102(b) imposes specific requirements upon the Secretary of Homeland Security to construct reinforced fencing along the southwest border. The nature of these requirements has changed over the years, including to expand the mileage along the border where fencing must be installed, and to afford the Secretary greater discretion in determining the type of fencing that may be employed and the particular location where fencing shall be installed.

Original Requirement to Augment the San Diego Border Fence

IIRIRA Section 102(b) directed immigration authorities to supplement the already existing 14- mile primary border fence near San Diego with two additional layers of fencing.[33] Environmental concerns and litigation resulted in significant delays in fulfilling this requirement. Over eight years after IIRIRA was enacted, DHS had not completed the fencing project.[34]

As discussed later in this report,[35] subsequent expansion of the Secretary of Homeland Security's authority to waive legal requirements that impeded construction of fencing projects, facilitated DHS's efforts to complete a second layer of fencing along the San Diego border.[36] Other amendments made to IIRIRA, discussed below, removed the statutory requirement that DHS complete the San Diego fencing project that had been authorized by IIRIRA when it was originally enacted in 1996.[37]

Expansion of Fencing Requirements under the Secure Fence Act of 2006

IIRIRA Section 102(b) was substantially revised by the Secure Fence Act of 2006.[38] Section 102(b)'s original requirement concerning fencing in the San Diego area was replaced with a much more expansive instruction to deploy "at least 2 layers of reinforced fencing, [and] the installation of additional physical barriers, roads, lighting, cameras, and sensors" along five specified stretches of the southwest border.[39] CBP estimated that this mandate covered roughly 850 miles.[40] The fencing mandate imposed by the Secure Fence Act was somewhat limited by a specification that "other means" could be used to secure an area where "the topography... has an elevation grade that exceeds 10 percent ..."[41]

In addition to this general mandate, the Secure Fence Act also provided deadlines for the completion of certain border projects. In particular, the act amended IIRIRA Section 102(b) to designate a stretch of border between Calexico, CA, and Douglas, AZ, as a priority area. It directed DHS to ensure that "an interlocking surveillance camera system" would be installed along this area by May 30, 2007, and to provide for the completion of fencing along this stretch by May 30, 2008.[42] A separate 30-mile stretch of fencing near Laredo, TX, was required to be deployed by December 31, 2008.[43] No timetable was specified, however, for DHS to complete double-layered fencing in the remaining stretches of the border.

Modification of Fencing Requirements Pursuant to the Consolidated Appropriations Act, 2008

The most recent revisions to IIRIRA Section 102 were enacted slightly more than a year after Congress passed the Secure Fence Act (and prior to the statutory deadlines for the deployment of double-layered fencing under the earlier act). The Consolidated Appropriations Act, 2008 (2008 Appropriations Act) amended IIRIRA Section 102(b) to significantly increase the Secretary of Homeland Security's discretion as to where to construct fencing along the southwest border. In particular, the 2008 Appropriations Act modified IIRIRA Section 102(b) in four ways:

- *Eliminated earlier requirement of double-layered fencing*—Whereas the prior language of IIRIRA Section 102(b), as amended by the Secure Fence Act, had generally required "at least 2 layers of reinforced fencing" be deployed in specified areas, Section 102(b) now mandates only a single layer of reinforced fencing (while not precluding additional layers from being deployed, if deemed appropriate).
- *Provided more flexible requirements concerning location of fencing and other border infrastructure*—While the Secure Fence Act required fencing to be installed along specific stretches of the southwest border, potentially totaling roughly 850 miles, the 2008 Appropriations Act replaced this specification with a more general requirement that fencing be deployed "along not less than 700 miles of the southwest border where fencing would be most practical and effective."[44] DHS was also instructed to construct "additional physical barriers, roads, lighting, cameras, and sensors to gain operational control of the southwest border." The Appropriations Act also amended IIRIRA Section 102(b) to provide that the Secretary was not obligated to deploy fencing or other border security infrastructure "in a particular location along an international border of the United States, if the Secretary determines that the use or placement of such resources is not the most appropriate means to achieve and maintain operational control over the international border at such location."[45]
- *New deadline for construction of fencing in "priority areas"*—The earlier version of IIRIRA Section 102(b) required the construction of fencing along specified stretches of the border, totaling roughly 370 miles, by May 2008, and fencing along another 30-mile section by December 2008.[46] This was replaced with a new requirement that the

Secretary of Homeland Security identify 370 miles "or other mileage" along the southwest border where fencing would be "most practical and effective," and complete construction of such fencing by December 31, 2008.[47]

- *New consultation requirements*—As amended, Section 102(b) of IIRIRA now requires the Secretary to consult with the Secretaries of the Interior and Agriculture, state and local governments, Indian tribes, and property owners "to minimize the impact on the environment, culture, commerce, and quality of life" in areas near where fencing is to be constructed.[48] The provision further provides that this consultation requirement does not create or negate any right to legal action by an affected person or entity.[49]

Select Issues Concerning Current IIRIRA Section 102(b)

As noted above, the 2008 Appropriations Act substantially modified IIRIRA Section 102(b) just over a year after the Secure Fence Act had done the same. These revisions, along with sometimes conflicting statements made by DHS officials to Congress concerning the agency's interpretation of its duties under Section 102(b), have potentially contributed to some disagreement regarding the nature of DHS's obligations under IIRIRA Section 102(b). The following paragraphs detail the legislative history of the most recent revisions to IIRIRA Section 102(b), the key elements of the requirements it imposes, and potential constraints on judicial review of DHS implementation of the statute's fencing requirements.

Legislative History

The legislative history behind the 2008 Appropriations Act's amendment to IIRIRA Section 102(b) is convoluted, and the explanatory materials for the enacted omnibus do not elaborate upon the amendment's purpose.[50] Nonetheless, materials in the *Congressional Record* may shed some light as to the sponsors' intended purpose, along with the context in which the proposed amendment was being considered.

The modifications to IIRIRA Section 102(b) appear to derive from language originally contained in a floor amendment offered during Senate consideration of the FY2008 homeland security appropriations bill. The floor amendment, offered by Senator Lindsey Graham and co-sponsored by a number of other Senators, would have added a new division entitled the "Border Security First Act of 2007" to the appropriations legislation.[51] In addition to modifying the fencing requirements contained in IIRIRA Section

102(b), the amendment would have required the deployment of 300 miles of vehicle barriers and 700 linear miles of fencing along the U.S.- Mexico border within two years; provided additional resources and requirements for DHS immigration enforcement programs at the border and within the interior of the United States; and made several substantive changes to the Immigration and Nationality Act and the U.S. Criminal Code.[52]

Senator Graham and a number of co-sponsors thereafter spoke in favor of the amendment, with three Senators specifically commenting upon the amendment's fencing provisions. Both Senator Graham and Senator Jeff Sessions, an amendment co-sponsor, characterized the amendment as providing for 700 miles of border fencing.[53] Senator John Cornyn, another co-sponsor, highlighted the amendment's proposed change to IIRIRA Section 102(b) as ensuring that DHS consulted with local officials and property owners regarding proposed fencing in a given area.[54]

The proposed amendment was later ruled by the Senate chair to be out of order, because some topics of the amendment were deemed non-germane to the appropriations bill being considered.[55]

The following day, Senator Graham offered a new amendment that was more limited in scope.[56] The new amendment did not include the original amendment's proposed modification of IIRIRA Section 102(b), or those provisions of the earlier amendment that would have substantively modified federal immigration and criminal statutes. However, the new amendment contained the earlier version's provision requiring DHS to deploy 300 miles of vehicle barriers and 700 linear miles of fencing along the southwest border within two years, along with a related provision appropriating funds for the completion of this project.[57] The amendment to the homeland security appropriations bill was adopted by a vote of 89-1.[58]

Separately, Senator Patty Murray offered an amendment on behalf of Senator Kay Bailey Hutchison to revise IIRIRA Section 102(b).[59] The revisions proposed in the Hutchison amendment were for the most part identical to those found in the amendment offered by Senator Graham the previous day.[60] The Hutchison amendment was approved by a voice vote,[61] and both it and the second Graham amendment (which Senator Hutchison also co-sponsored)[62] were included in the Senate-passed version of the homeland security appropriations bill.[63]

Later in the year, 11 regular appropriations measures for FY2008, including appropriations for homeland security, were combined into an omnibus bill that became the 2008 Appropriations Act.[64] The omnibus legislation reconciled differences between the competing House- and Senate-passed homeland security appropriations bills. The final act included the provision in the Senate-passed bill that revised IIRIRA Section 102(b), which had been added by the Hutchison amendment.[65] However, the final act did not retain the Senate-passed bill's provisions that had been added by the Graham amendment, which would have separately imposed a two-year deadline for the completion of 700 linear miles of fencing and 300 miles of vehicle barriers, and provided appropriations to ensure that these deadlines were met.[66]

Type of Fencing Required under Current Law

The 2008 Appropriations Act amended IIRIRA in a manner that provides DHS with significant discretion as to the manner in which to install fencing—undoing some of the more specific requirements that had previously been imposed. Whereas the Secure Fence Act had amended IIRIRA Section 102(b) to provide that "at least 2 layers of reinforced fencing" were to be installed along specified stretches of the border, the 2008 Appropriations Act replaced this with a more general requirement that "reinforced fencing" be installed along the southwest border. In other words, IIRIRA Section 102(b) no longer requires DHS to install two or more layers of reinforced fencing at any location along the border—a single layer of reinforced fencing appears sufficient to satisfy the statutory mandate. DHS would appear to have discretion to construct additional layers of fencing pursuant to its general authority under IIRIRA Section 102(a), however, if it deems such fencing to be appropriate.[67]

Some disagreement has arisen over DHS's use of "vehicle fencing" to satisfy IIRIRA's fencing requirements.[68] Vehicle fencing is a type of barrier designed to inhibit the illegal crossing of vehicles into the United States, but not pedestrians.[69] Some Members of Congress have argued that the "fencing" referred to in IIRIRA Section 102 should be limited to the type that is effective at preventing all illegal entrants, whether traveling by vehicle or by foot.[70]

On the other hand, IIRIRA Section 102(b) does not mandate that any particular type of fencing must be deployed, beyond providing that such fencing be "reinforced."[71] The statute does not specify, for example, that deployed fencing must be of a particular height, or be constructed in a particular style (e.g., using bollard, wire mesh, or chain link).[72] In the absence of language specifying the use of a particular kind of fencing,[73] it would appear that DHS enjoys broad discretion to assess the appropriate type of fencing to deploy in order to achieve operational control of the southwest border.

Miles Along the Border vs. Total Miles of Fencing

While IIRIRA Section 102(b) is sometimes characterized as requiring DHS to deploy "700 miles of fencing," the express language of the text seems to indicate that DHS's mandate is somewhat distinct. Section 102(b) requires DHS to deploy fencing "along not less than 700 miles of the southwest border." This seems to be a somewhat different requirement, which prioritizes the actual mileage of the border covered by fencing, rather than just the number of miles of fencing deployed. For example, if DHS hypothetically deployed 30 miles of fencing, but did so through the construction of a 10-layered, 3-mile-long fence, it would have only installed fencing along 3 miles of the border. On the other hand, if DHS deployed such fencing in a single layer of fencing, it would have deployed fencing along 30 miles of the border.

Likely because of the phraseology of IIRIRA Section 102(b), DHS seems to only count the mileage of primary layers of fencing deployed along the southwest border when discussing its efforts to satisfy its statutory mandate, and not the total amount of fencing that it has deployed (i.e., including secondary and tertiary layers of fencing that run behind some stretches of primary fencings).[74]

Priority Fencing Mandate

As amended by the 2008 Appropriations Act, IIRIRA 102(b) contains two distinct but related mandates. One of the mandates, which can be referred to as the *priority fencing mandate*, required DHS to identify and complete construction of fencing in priority areas of the southwest border by December 31, 2008. The second mandate, which can be referred to as the *general fencing mandate*, requires reinforced fencing to be deployed along "not less than 700 miles" of the southwest border, but contained no deadline for deployment.[75] The *general fencing mandate* is subject to a proviso that DHS is not required to install fencing or other infrastructure "at any particular location" along the border, if the use or placement of fencing at that location is not deemed by the Secretary of Homeland Security to be the most appropriate means to achieve and maintain control.

Section 102(b)'s *priority fencing mandate* required DHS, before December 31, 2008, to identify either 370 miles "or other mileage" along the southwest border where fencing would be most appropriate to deter unlawful migration and smuggling activities. Construction of the identified fencing was required to have also been completed by the end of 2008. Although DHS initially planned to deploy 670 miles of fencing pursuant to this mandate,[76] it subsequently revised these plans prior to the reaching the deadline for priority fence construction.[77] According to a 2010 report by the Government Accountability Office (GAO), DHS opted to comply with the *priority fencing mandate* by ensuring that reinforced fencing had been deployed along 370 miles of the southwest border.[78]

General Fencing Mandate

Although the *priority fencing mandate* of IIRIRA Section 102(b) has been satisfied, the *general fencing mandate* has not yet been fulfilled. DHS has thus far deployed reinforced fencing along roughly 653 miles of the border.[79] At least on first look, it would appear that the agency would need to install additional fencing along nearly 50 miles of the southwest border to meet the requirements of Section 102(b).

There have been conflicting views among some policymakers as to the firmness of the *general fencing mandate*. Although one clause of IIRIRA Section 102(b) requires fencing "along not less than 700 miles" of the border, another clause in that subsection provides:

> Notwithstanding [the *general fencing mandate* of this section] nothing in this paragraph shall require the Secretary of Homeland Security to install fencing, physical barriers, roads, lighting, cameras, and sensors in a particular location along an international border of the United States, if the Secretary determines that the use or placement of such resources is not the most appropriate means to achieve and maintain operational control over the international border at such location.[80]

The meaning and effect of this proviso is arguably open to interpretation. One way to read the clause is simply to reflect the discretion that Congress intended to afford DHS in determining where to deploy at least 700 miles of fencing along the southwest border. As discussed previously, prior to amendments made by the 2008 Appropriations Act, the subsection had required DHS to deploy fencing along specific stretches of the southwest border that were identified within the statutory command.[81] The new proviso could be interpreted to emphasize the discretion that DHS was afforded as a result of the revisions made by the 2008 Appropriations Act. While DHS is required to construct fencing along at least 700 miles of the border, the agency retains discretion to determine the most appropriate stretches along the 1,933 mile-land border where the fencing should be deployed.

Relatedly, the "notwithstanding" proviso to *the general fencing mandate* affords a potential response to claims that DHS did not place fencing at a location where it would be "most practical and effective." DHS is not required to install fencing at a location if "the Secretary determines that the placement of such resources is not the most appropriate means to achieve and maintain operational control ... at such location."[82] This is phrased in a manner that suggests that the Secretary's determination not to place fencing at a location would be afforded a very high degree of deference by a reviewing court.[83] In other words, the "notwithstanding" clause enables DHS to readily answer claims by parties seeking to compel some portion of the required border fencing at a location where the fencing would allegedly be "most practical and effective." Arguably, however, the proviso could be interpreted more broadly, to signify something other than simply the discretion that DHS possesses in determining the stretches of the border along which to construct fencing. Although the proviso is not crafted as an express waiver,[84] the clause's usage of "notwithstanding" could be construed to supersede any conflicting requirements imposed by the *general fencing mandate*.[85] Under a broad interpretation of the "notwithstanding" proviso, it might be argued that the Secretary is not necessarily required to deploy fencing along 700 miles of the border, if the Secretary concludes that fencing is the appropriate means of achieving operational control along a lesser mileage of the border.

There are difficulties, however, with interpreting the "notwithstanding" proviso so broadly. As an initial matter, the proviso does not expressly state that DHS may opt to construct a lesser amount of fencing than is specified elsewhere in Section 102(b). Rather, the proviso states that DHS is not required to construct fencing "at a particular location," if the Secretary of Homeland Security determines that the installation of that infrastructure is not appropriate for "such location." As noted above, this provision could reasonably be construed to mean that, in carrying out its *general fencing mandate* to deploy fencing along 700 miles of the southwest border, DHS is not legally required to install any portion of this required fencing at "any particular location."

The ability to construe the proviso in more than one way may be significant. Courts typically follow the interpretive principle that a "statute should be construed so that effect is given to all its provisions, so that no part will be inoperative or superfluous, void or insignificant.... "[86] If Section 102(b)'s proviso is construed to mean that DHS is only required to deploy the amount of fencing along the border that it deems appropriate, the clause would render Section 102(b)'s mandate that fencing be deployed "along at least 700 miles of the border" superfluous. On the other hand, if the proviso is interpreted to mean that, in carrying out its mandate to construct fencing along at least 700 miles of the border the border, DHS is not legally required to install the required fencing at any particular location, every provision of IIRIRA Section 102(b) can be given effect.

The legislative history behind IIRIRA Section 102(b)'s fencing requirements also seems to support a narrow construction of Section 102(b)'s "notwithstanding" clause. As discussed previously, the amendments made to IIRIRA Section 102(b) by the 2008 Appropriations Act were originally part of a package of amendments, approved by the Senate as part of a homeland security appropriations bill, which were intended to ensure that fencing along 700 miles of the border would be constructed expeditiously.[87] The legislative history of these amendments' consideration, along with their plain text, seems to indicate that the amendments' purpose was to ensure that fencing was deployed along 700 miles of the border within two years. Indeed, the Senator who offered the amendment to IIRIRA Section 102(b) also co-sponsored these related amendments.[88] While Congress ultimately opted to enact one of these amendments into law but not the other, presumably the Senate would not have originally approved both amendments if they were understood to be conflicting.

To date, it appears that every federal court which has discussed IIRIRA Section 102(b) has described the provision in mandatory terms: DHS is required to deploy fencing along 700 miles of the southwest border, but it retains discretion to determine the appropriate locations in which to deploy the required fencing.[89] It should be noted, however, that no court has definitively ruled that an alternative interpretation is not permissible, or closely examined the interplay between the "notwithstanding" proviso and the general fencing requirement. But the uniform interpretation may suggest that, as a matter of first impression, Section 102(b) may be most reasonably construed as establishing a mandate to deploy fencing along at least 700 miles of the border.

For its part, DHS has appeared to take conflicting views regarding the firmness of IIRIRA Section 102(b)'s *general fencing mandate*. Initially, DHS appeared to construe the 700-mile requirement as a firm requirement. In notices issued in the *Federal Register* in 2008 describing border fencing projects undertaken under IIRIRA Section 102(b), Secretary of Homeland Security Michael Chertoff stated that "Congress has called for the installation of fencing, barriers, roads, lighting, cameras, and sensors on not less than 700 miles of the southwest border...."[90]

In March 2009, Secretary of Homeland Security Janet Napolitano wrote to the House Homeland Security Committee in response to questions regarding DHS's obligations to deploy fencing along the southwest border. Secretary

Napolitano described IIRIRA as mandating that DHS construct at least 700 miles of fencing, but at least for the immediate future, DHS would focus on fence deployment in priority areas:

> As amended, the Act mandates the completion of 700 total miles of fence. It also mandates that the Secretary identify priority areas "where fencing would be the most practical and effective in deterring smugglers and aliens attempting to gain illegal entry into the United States." As of March 6, 2009, DHS has completed approximately 611 of the 661 miles of fence identified by the Border Patrol as priority areas. While fencing remains an important tool in achieving effective control, it is only one element of our overall border security strategy that incorporates the proper mix of technology personnel, and tactical infrastructure. Currently, there are no immediate funded plans to construct additional fencing.[91]

DHS later appeared to modify its interpretation of the IIRIRA Section 102(b), and began to describe the "notwithstanding" proviso as permitting it to deploy fencing along less than 700 miles of the border, if the agency deemed a lesser amount of fencing to be appropriate to achieve operational control.[92] Indeed, four years after describing IIRIRA Section 102(b) as imposing a firm mandate, Secretary Napolitano gave testimony before the Senate Judiciary Committee in which she appeared to take the view that DHS was legally permitted to construct a lesser amount of fencing.[93]

To date, DHS has not publicly released a formal legal opinion describing its interpretation of the fencing mandate established by IIRIRA Section 102(b), or announced whether or how its opinion has changed over the years. In defending DHS against a legal challenge by the State of Arizona in 2011,[94] in which Arizona sought to compel DHS to complete construction of fencing along 700 miles of the border (and undertake other immigration enforcement actions), the Department of Justice did not dispute the existence of this mandate, but instead argued that DHS decisions as to where to locate such fencing and the speed by which fencing was to deployed were committed to agency discretion.[95]

It should be noted that, in assessing the permissibility of an agency's interpretation of the laws it administers, reviewing courts typically accord the agency's interpretation of these statutes with some degree of deference, so long as the construction is reasonable.[96] In determining whether an agency's construction of a statute is reasonable, legislative intent is a touchstone for a reviewing court's analysis—an agency's interpretation might be entitled to deference when congressional intent is ambiguous and the agency's construction of the statute is reasonable.[97] Moreover, agency interpretations of statutory requirements are usually afforded a lesser degree of deference when the agency interpretation is not the result of a notice-and-comment rulemaking process or formal adjudication.[98] In such circumstances, the level of deference given to the agency's interpretation "will depend upon the thoroughness evident in its consideration, the validity of its reasoning, its consistency with earlier and later pronouncements, and all those factors which give it power to persuade, if lacking power to control."[99] The appropriate degree of deference to which DHS's interpretation of the statutory requirements imposed by IIRIRA should be afforded may be subject to differing views.[100]

Assuming that DHS's interpretation of the requirements under IIRIRA Section 102(b) is subject to legal challenge, the degree of deference that a reviewing court gives to the agency's interpretation may be informed by a number of factors, including whether (1) the plain text of the statute is ambiguous, and DHS's interpretation is reasonable; (2) other indicia of legislative intent favor a particular interpretation; and (3) the agency's apparent modification of its interpretation of IIRIRA Section 102(b) entitles its current interpretation to a lesser degree of deference.

Potential Constraints on Judicial Review

Regardless of the appropriate interpretation of Section 102(b)'s general fencing mandate and the "notwithstanding" proviso, the statute imposes no clear deadline for when the contemplated fencing must be deployed. In the 2011 litigation in which Arizona sought to compel DHS to complete construction of fencing required under IIRIRA Section 102(b), the reviewing federal district court dismissed Arizona's motion, in part because "no deadline mandates completion of the fencing and infrastructure developments or any required discrete action by a specified time."[101] The court further observed that, although "the construction of the fencing and infrastructure improvements may be phrased in mandatory language," IIRIRA affords DHS "a great deal of discretion in deciding how, when, and where to complete the construction."[102]

The absence of a deadline for the completion of the fencing requirements of IIRIRA Section 102(b) does not necessarily mean that DHS has no judicially enforceable legal obligation to complete any remaining fencing. The Administrative Procedure Act (APA), for example, provides courts with the authority to compel agency action, when such action has been "unlawfully withheld or unreasonably delayed."[103] Determining whether an agency has unreasonably delayed undertaking a required action is a fact-specific determination made on a case-by-case basis, with reviewing courts typically showing more deference to an agency when there is not a statutory deadline for agency action.[104]

If a court determined that DHS had unreasonably delayed fulfillment of its obligations under IIRIRA Section 102(b), it might deem the completion of at least 700 miles of fence along the southwest border to constitute "a discrete agency action" that it would potentially have the power to compel.[105] The district court in the *Arizona* case found that completion of the border fence was not a "discrete agency action" that it could compel DHS to take, but it did not explain the basis for this conclusion.[106]

Moreover, even assuming that a court might have jurisdiction to review a claim that DHS unreasonably delayed fence construction, it is not clear who would have standing to make such a claim.[107] To demonstrate standing, a plaintiff must (1) show a concrete and particularized, actual or imminent injury; (2) demonstrate a fairly traceable, causal connection between the injury and the defendant's conduct; and (3) demonstrate that it is likely that the injury will be redressed by a favorable court decision. It may be difficult for a plaintiff to identify a concrete, particularized injury that would be effectively remedied if DHS deployed fencing along an additional 50 miles of the border. In the *Arizona* case, the district court presumed without deciding that Arizona had standing, but dismissed its claims.[108]

Authority to Waive Legal Requirements Impeding Construction of Roads and Barriers

Section 102(c) of IIRIRA confers the Secretary of Homeland Security with broad authority to waive legal requirements that may impede the construction of barriers and roads along the border. The nature and scope of this waiver authority changed significantly pursuant to modifications made by the REAL ID Act of 2005. In the years following, the Secretary of Homeland Security employed this waiver authority to facilitate the construction of hundreds of miles of fencing and other infrastructure along several sections of the southwest border. More recently, however, this waiver authority has not been employed to facilitate further large-scale border projects.

Original Waiver Authority

When initially enacted in 1996, IIRIRA Section 102(c) expressly authorized the waiver the Endangered Species Act (ESA) and the National Environmental Policy Act (NEPA),[109] to the extent that such waivers were determined necessary by the Attorney General to expeditiously construct barriers and roads under Section 102. Other federal laws, however, remained applicable to border construction projects. Federal immigration authorities appear to have not employed IIRIRA Section 102(c), as originally enacted, to waive NEPA and ESA requirements.[110]

In 2004, eight years after IIRIRA mandated completion of a second and third layer of fencing along the San Diego border, fencing was still not completed due to litigation and concerns related to environmental statutes other than NEPA and the ESA.[111] The California Coastal Commission essentially halted the San Diego fencing project after determining that DHS had not demonstrated, among other things, that the project was consistent "to the maximum extent practicable" with the policies of the California Coastal Management Program—a state program approved under the federal Coastal Zone Management Act, 16 U.S.C. §§1451, *et seq.*[112]

Expansion of Waiver Authority under the REAL ID Act

In part due to delays in the construction of fencing near San Diego,[113] Congress amended IIRIRA Section 102(c) via the REAL ID Act of 2005. As amended, IIRIRA Section 102(c) permits the Secretary of DHS to waive "all legal requirements" necessary to ensure expeditious construction of these security barriers.[114] Such waivers are effective upon publication in the *Federal Register.*[115] Federal district courts are provided with exclusive jurisdiction to review claims alleging that the actions or decisions of the Secretary violate the U.S. Constitution, and district court rulings may be reviewed only by the Supreme Court, whose review is discretionary.

The scope of this waiver authority is substantial—with some observers describing it as possibly having greater reach than any other waiver authority conferred by statute[116]—leading some to express concern over its breadth and the limited scope of judicial review available for waiver decisions.[117] Although IIRIRA Section 102(c), as amended by the REAL ID Act, could not properly be construed to permit the Secretary to waive application of the Constitution to fencing projects,[118] the waiver potentially could be employed with respect to any other existing legal requirement—provided that the Secretary of Homeland Security concluded that compliance with the requirement would impede expeditious construction of barriers and roads. Waivers issued under

IIRIRA Section 102(c) have not only targeted federal and state statutes, but also any regulations and requirements deriving from or relating to such laws.

Nonetheless, the waiver authority conferred by IIRIRA Section 102(c) is not absolute. The Secretary may only waive those legal requirements that, in effect, would impede the construction of barriers and roads under Section 102. The authority does not appear to permit the Secretary to waive legal requirements that only tangentially relate to, or do not necessarily interfere with, the construction of roads and barriers.[119] The decision of whether to waive a legal requirement is the responsibility of the Secretary of Homeland Security, and authority may be exercised in his discretion. Until such time as the Secretary waives an applicable law, however, DHS must generally follow all legal requirements normally imposed on federal agencies.[120]

To date, the Secretary of DHS has provided notice in the *Federal Register* on five occasions that he was invoking the waiver authority conferred under IIRIRA Section 102(c):

- *San Diego Border Sector*—On September 22, 2005, a notice was issued in the *Federal Register* indicating that waiver authority had been exercised over various legal requirements in order to ensure the expeditious construction of the San Diego border fence.[121] The waiver applies to "all federal, state, or other laws, regulations and legal requirements of, deriving from, or related to the subject," of various federal statutes listed in *Appendix B*.
- *Barry M. Goldwater Range (BMGR) in Southwestern Arizona*—A *Federal Register* notice was published on January 19, 2007, indicating that the Secretary was waiving various legal requirements in order to ensure the expeditious construction of physical barriers and roads in the vicinity of the BMGR in southwestern Arizona.[122] The waiver applies to all "[f]ederal, [s]tate, or other laws, regulations and legal requirements of, deriving from, or related to the subject" of several federal statutes listed in *Appendix C*.
- *San Pedro Riparian National Conservation Area in Southeastern Arizona*— On October 5, 2007, Defenders of Wildlife and the Sierra Club brought suit seeking a temporary restraining order (TRO) enjoining DHS from border fence and road-building activities in the San Pedro Riparian National Conservation Area, located in the vicinity of the U.S. border in southeastern Arizona.[123] On October 10, 2007, the presiding district court judge issued a TRO halting fence construction activities in the Conservation Area, finding the

relevant federal agencies had failed to carry out an environmental assessment as legally required under NEPA.[124] On October 26, 2007, a notice was published in the *Federal Register* indicating that the Secretary of Homeland Security had exercised waiver authority over various legal requirements in order to ensure the expeditious construction of physical barriers or roads through the San Pedro Riparian National Conservation Area (including any and all lands covered by the TRO),[125] thereby enabling the DHS to resume fence construction. The waiver applies to "all federal, state, or other laws, regulations and legal requirements of, deriving from, or related to the subject" of a collection of federal statutes listed in *Appendix D.*

- *Hidalgo County, Texas*—On April 3, 2008, notice was given in the *Federal Register* that the Secretary of Homeland Security had exercised his waiver authority under IIRIRA Section 102(c) to ensure the construction of barriers and roads in Hidalgo County, Texas.[126] The waiver applies to "all federal, state, or other laws, regulations and legal requirements of, deriving from, or related to the subject" of various federal statutes listed in *Appendix E.*
- *Border Projects in California, Arizona, New Mexico, and Texas*—On April 3, 2008, the Secretary of Homeland Security gave notice in the *Federal Register* of the waiver of various laws in relation to border construction projects in California, Arizona, New Mexico, and Texas.[127] The waiver applies to "all federal, state, or other laws, regulations and legal requirements of, deriving from, or related to the subject" of various federal statutes listed in *Appendix F.*

In multiple instances, lawsuits were brought challenging the constitutionality of an issued waiver. Constitutional claims raised in these collective cases included arguments that the waiver authority was an impermissible delegation of Congress's lawmaking authority; the waiver provision violated the Presentment Clause by effectively enabling the executive branch to "repeal" or "amend" existing laws to exempt border infrastructure projects from their coverage; and the waiver authority's application to state and local laws violated federalism and anti-commandeering principles. In each case, the reviewing federal district court upheld the exercise of waiver authority as constitutionally valid.[128] Parties in two of the cases sought Supreme Court review, but the Court declined to grant certiorari in either case.[129]

CONCLUSION

Pursuant to IIRIRA Section 102, Congress has conferred DHS with clear authority to construct barriers and roads along the international land borders to deter illegal crossings in areas of high illegal entry. More specifically, it has required fencing to be constructed along specified mileage of the southwest border. In recent years, legislative attention has primarily focused upon the fencing requirements contained in IIRIRA Section 102(b). Prior versions of Section 102(b) imposed specific requirements as to the location where fencing was to be installed and the layers of fencing to be constructed. The current provision affords DHS with significantly greater discretion to determine the appropriate location, layers, and types of fencing to be installed along the southwest border.

Whether DHS has discretion to construct less fencing than the amount specified under IIRIRA Section 102(b), on account of a proviso that posits that the agency is not required to construct fencing at any "particular location" where it deems fencing to be inappropriate, has been the subject of disagreement (and apparently inconsistent views by DHS itself). While there appears to be stronger support for construing Section 102(b) to establish a firm mandate for the deployment of fencing along 700 miles of the border, with the agency retaining discretion as to the locations along the border where fencing should be installed, it is not clear whether a court would have the ability to compel DHS to install additional fencing (or that a plaintiff would have standing to bring such a claim). If Congress disagrees with DHS's implementation of the fencing mandate under Section 102(b), it would likely need to enact legislation to modify or clarify the fencing requirements found in current statute.

But even assuming that DHS satisfies the fencing requirements under Section 102(b), the general authority conferred to the agency under Section 102(a) permits it to construct additional fencing or other barriers along the U.S. land borders. There is nothing in current statute that would bar DHS from potentially installing hundreds of miles of additional fencing along the border, at least so long as the action was determined appropriate to deter illegal crossings in areas of high illegal entry. Moreover, IIRIRA Section 102(c) grants DHS authority to waive any legal requirement that would impede the expeditious construction of additional barriers and roads. DHS's decision not to deploy a substantial amount of additional fencing, beyond what is required under IIRIRA Section 102(b), appears primarily premised on policy considerations and funding constraints, rather than significant legal impediments. Accordingly, policymakers may deem it appropriate to review and assess the scope of DHS's authority to construct barriers, and the manner in which such authority is exercised, even after any requirements under IIRIRA Section 102(b) are satisfied.

APPENDIX A. IIRIRA SECTION 102, AS AMENDED (TEXT)[130]

Sec. 102 - Improvement of Barriers at Border

(a)In General.-The Secretary of Homeland Security shall take such actions as may be necessary to install additional physical barriers and roads (including the removal of obstacles to detection of illegal entrants) in the vicinity of the United States border to deter illegal crossings in areas of high illegal entry into the United States.

(b)Construction of Fencing and Road Improvements Along the Border.-

(1) Additional fencing along southwest border.-

(A) Reinforced fencing.-In carrying out subsection (a), the Secretary of Homeland Security shall construct reinforced fencing along not less than 700 miles of the southwest border where fencing would be most practical and effective and provide for the installation of additional physical barriers, roads, lighting, cameras, and sensors to gain operational control of the southwest border.

(B) Priority areas.-In carrying out this section [amending this section], the Secretary of Homeland Security shall-

(i)identify the 370 miles, or other mileage determined by the Secretary, whose authority to determine other mileage shall expire on December 31, 2008, along the southwest border where fencing would be most practical and effective in deterring smugglers and aliens attempting to gain illegal entry into the United States; and

(ii)not later than December 31, 2008, complete construction of reinforced fencing along the miles identified under clause (i).

(C) Consultation.-

(i)In general.-In carrying out this section, the Secretary of Homeland Security shall consult with the Secretary of the Interior, the Secretary of Agriculture, States, local governments, Indian tribes, and property owners in the United States to minimize the impact on the environment, culture, commerce, and quality of life for the communities and residents located near the sites at which such fencing is to be constructed.

(ii)Savings provision.-Nothing in this subparagraph may be construed to-

(I) create or negate any right of action for a State, local government, or other person or entity affected by this subsection; or

(II) affect the eminent domain laws of the United States or of any State.

(D) Limitation on requirements.-Notwithstanding subparagraph (A), nothing in this paragraph shall require the Secretary of Homeland Security to install fencing, physical barriers, roads, lighting, cameras, and sensors in a particular location along an international border of the United States, if the Secretary determines that the use or placement of such resources is not the most appropriate means to achieve and maintain operational control over the international border at such location.

(2) Prompt acquisition of necessary easements.-The Attorney General, acting under the authority conferred in section 103(b) of the Immigration and Nationality Act [8 U.S.C. 1103(b)] (as inserted by subsection (d)), shall promptly acquire such easements as may be necessary to carry out this subsection and shall commence construction of fences immediately following such acquisition (or conclusion of portions thereof).

(3) Safety features.-The Attorney General, while constructing the additional fencing under this subsection, shall incorporate such safety features into the design of the fence system as are necessary to ensure the well-being of border patrol agents deployed within or in near proximity to the system.

(4) Authorization of appropriations.-There are authorized to be appropriated such sums as may be necessary to carry out this subsection. Amounts appropriated under this paragraph are authorized to remain available until expended.

(c) Waiver.-

(1) In general.-Notwithstanding any other provision of law, the Secretary of Homeland Security shall have the authority to waive all legal requirements such Secretary, in such Secretary's sole discretion, determines necessary to ensure expeditious construction of the barriers and roads under this section [amending this section]. Any such decision by the Secretary shall be effective upon being published in the Federal Register.

(2) Federal court review.-

(A) In general.-The district courts of the United States shall have exclusive jurisdiction to hear all causes or claims arising from any action undertaken, or any decision made, by the Secretary of Homeland Security pursuant to paragraph (1). A cause of action or claim may only be brought alleging a violation of the Constitution of the United States. The court shall not have jurisdiction to hear any claim not specified in this subparagraph.

(B)Time for filing of complaint.-Any cause or claim brought pursuant to subparagraph (A) shall be filed not later than 60 days after the date of the action or decision made by the Secretary of Homeland Security. A claim shall be barred unless it is filed within the time specified.

(C) Ability to seek appellate review.-An interlocutory or final judgment, decree, or order of the district court may be reviewed only upon petition for a writ of certiorari to the Supreme Court of the United States.

APPENDIX B. LEGAL REQUIREMENTS WAIVED BY DHS FOR THE CONSTRUCTION OF THE SAN DIEGO BORDER FENCE

Laws Waived	Pertinent Requirements
Administrative Procedure Act (APA) 5 U.S.C. §§551 et seq.	The APA establishes the general procedures that an agency must follow when promulgating a legislative rule. An agency must publish a notice of proposed rulemaking in the Federal Register, afford interested persons an opportunity to participate in the proceeding through the submission of written comments or, at the discretion of the agency, by oral presentation, and when consideration of the matter is completed, incorporate in the rules adopted "a concise general statement of their basis and purpose." A final rule must be published in the Federal Register "not less than 30 days before its effective date."
Clean Air Act (CAA) 42 U.S.C. §§7401 et seq.	The CAA requires the Environmental Protection Agency to establish minimum national standards for air quality, known as National Ambient Air Quality Standards (NAAQS), and assigns primary responsibility to the states to assure compliance with the standards. Areas not meeting the standards, referred to as "nonattainment areas," are required to implement specified air pollution control measures. Federal agencies must comply with the federal general air conformity rule set forth by the CAA and codified in 40 CFR Part 51. The general conformity rule requires federal agencies to ensure that actions are consistent with the applicable state plan. The states administer the CAA through a comprehensive permitting program.
Coastal Zone Management Act (CZMA) 16 U.S.C.	The CZMA requires federal agency activity within or outside the coastal zone that affects any land or water use or natural

Laws Waived	Pertinent Requirements
§§1451 et seq.	resource of the coastal zone to be carried out in a manner that is consistent to the maximum extent practicable with the policies of an approved state management program. The federal agency must submit a consistency determination to the applicable state agency.
Endangered Species Act (ESA) 16 U.S.C. §§1531 et seq.	Section 7 of the ESA mandates that each federal agency consult with the Fish and Wildlife Service (FWS) or National Marine Fishery Services (NMFS), depending on the listed species involved, to ensure that its actions are "not likely to jeopardize the continued existence of any endangered species or threatened species, or result in the destruction or adverse modification of" designated critical habitat. Once consulted, FWS or NMFS must, if listed species might be affected, prepare a biological opinion related to the actual impact of the proposed action. Mitigation measures could be required.
Federal Water Pollution Control Act (Clean Water Act) 33 U.S.C. §§1251 et seq.	Section 404 of the Clean Water Act establishes a program to regulate the discharge of dredged or fill material into waters of the United States, including wetlands. Section 404 requires a permit before dredged or fill material may be discharged into waters of the United States, unless the activity is exempt.
Migratory Bird Treaty Act (MBTA) 16 U.S.C. §§703 et seq.	Section 2 of the MBTA sets out the types of prohibited conduct and states: "Unless and except as permitted by regulations ... it shall be unlawful at any time, by any means, or in any manner, to pursue, hunt, take, capture, kill, attempt to do these acts, [or] possess ... any migratory bird, [or] any part, nest, or eggs of any such bird.... " Violations of the MBTA may result in civil or criminal penalties.
National Environmental Policy Act (NEPA) 42 U.S.C. §§4321 et seq.	Under NEPA, an environmental impact statement must be prepared for "every recommendation or report on proposals for legislation and other major federal actions significantly affecting the quality of the human environment." NEPA regulations require that if an agency is uncertain whether an action's impacts on the environment will be significant, it generally must prepare an environmental assessment (EA). An EA is carried out to clarify issues and determine the extent of an action's environmental effects.
National Historic Preservation Act (NHPA) 16 U.S.C. §§470 et seq. (Act repealed by P.L. 113-287, §7; similar provisions now codified in Title 54 of the U.S. Code)	In accordance with the NHPA and its implementing regulations, sites determined to be eligible for inclusion in the National Register of Historic Places must be protected, either through avoidance or other mitigative action, from direct and indirect impacts. The NHPA also has procedural requirements, including public notice and comment.

APPENDIX C. LEGAL REQUIREMENTS WAIVED BY DHS FOR THE CONSTRUCTION OF PHYSICAL BARRIERS AND ROADS IN THE VICINITY OF THE BARRY M. GOLDWATER RANGE IN SOUTHWEST ARIZONA

Laws Waived	Pertinent Requirements
Administrative Procedure Act (APA) 5 U.S.C. §§551 et seq.	See Appendix B for description of requirements.
Endangered Species Act (ESA) 16 U.S.C. §§1531 et seq.	See Appendix B for description of requirements.
Federal Water Pollution Control Act (Clean Water Act) 33 U.S.C. §§1251 et seq.	See Appendix B for description of requirements.
Military Lands Withdrawal Act of 1999 P.L. 106-65, Div. B.	Section 3031 of the Military Lands Withdrawal Act of 1999 withdrew federal lands administered by the Bureau of Land Management from the public domain for 25 years, transferred these lands to the Secretaries of the Air Force and the Navy for this period, and reserved the lands for U.S. military training, testing, and other related purposes within the Barry M. Goldwater Range. The Secretaries of the Air Force, Navy, and Interior were required to prepare an Integrated Natural Resources Management Plan (INRMP) under the Sikes Act which, among other things, provided that "all gates, fences, and barriers constructed on such lands ... be designed and erected to allow wildlife access, to the extent practicable and consistent with military security, safety, and sound wildlife management use."
National Environmental Policy Act (NEPA) 42 U.S.C. §§4321 et seq.	See Appendix B for description of requirements.
National Historic Preservation Act (NHPA) 16 U.S.C. §§470 et seq. (Act repealed by P.L. 113-287, §7; similar provisions now codified in Title 54 of the U.S. Code)	See Appendix B for description of requirements.
National Wildlife Refuge System Administration Act 16 U.S.C. §§668dd-668ee.	The National Wildlife Refuge System (NWRS) was primarily established to ensure the conservation of fish, wildlife, and plants. Designated areas may be used for

Laws Waived	Pertinent Requirements
	other purposes (e.g., hunting, timber harvest, and grazing) only to the extent that such activities are compatible with the purposes for which the refuge was created. The refuges are managed by the Fish and Wildlife Service.
Sikes Act 16 U.S.C. §§670 et seq.	The Sikes Act requires the Secretary of Defense to carry out a program providing for the conservation and rehabilitation of natural resources on U.S. military installations under the jurisdiction of the Secretary (including federal lands withdrawn from the public domain, transferred to the Secretary, and reserved for U.S. military use). In cooperation with the Secretary of the Interior, the Secretary of each military department is required to prepare and implement an Integrated Natural Resources Management Plan (INRMP) for each military installation under the jurisdiction of that Secretary if the installation contains "significant" natural resources.
Wilderness Act 16 U.S.C. §§1131 et seq.	The Wilderness Act established a National Wilderness Preservation System on federal lands "where the earth and its community of life are untrammele by man, where man himself is a visitor who does not remain." Within designated wilderness areas, section 4(c) of the act generally prohibits structures or installations, motor vehicle or other forms of mechanical transport, and roads.

Appendix D. Legal Requirements Waived by DHS for the Construction of Physical Barriers and Roads in the Vicinity of the San Pedro Riparian National

Laws Waived	Pertinent Requirements
Administrative Procedure Act (APA) 5 U.S.C. §§551 et seq.	See Appendix B for description of requirements.
Antiquities Act 16 U.S.C. §§431 et seq. (Act repealed by P.L. 113-287, §7; similar provisions now codified in Title 54 of the U.S. Code)	The Antiquities Act authorizes the President to declare as national monuments federal lands that contain historic landmarks, historic and prehistoric structures, and other objects of historic or scientific interest. Other provisions authorize the Secretaries of the Interior, Agriculture, and Army to issue permits to qualified institutions for the excavation of archaeological sites and gathering of objects of antiquity on lands under their respective

Appendix D. (Continued)

Laws Waived	Pertinent Requirements
	jurisdictions. Penalties are provided for removing, excavating, or damaging resources protected under the act.
Archaeological and Historic Preservation Act (AHPA) 16 U.S.C. §§469 et seq.	The purpose of the AHPA is to provide for the preservation of historical and archeological data which might otherwise be irreparably lost or destroyed as the result of, among other things, any alteration of terrain caused by a federal construction project. If a federal agency becomes aware that its activities in connection with a construction project may cause irreparable loss or destruction of significant scientific, prehistorical, historical, or archeological data, the agency must notify the Secretary of the Interior. If the Secretary deems such data to be significant and in danger of being irrevocably lost or destroyed, he is authorized to take action to protect and recover it.
Archeological Resources Protection Act (ARPA) 16 U.S.C. §§470aa et seq.	ARPA generally prohibits the damage, removal, excavation, or alteration of any archeological resource located on public lands or Indian lands, except pursuant to a permit issued by the appropriate federal land manager.
Arizona-Idaho Conservation Act of 1988 16 U.S.C.§§460xx et seq.	The Arizona-Idaho Conservation Act established the San Pedro Riparian National Conservation Area to protect public lands surrounding the San Pedro River in Cochise County, Arizona. The Secretary of the Interior is responsible for managing the area in a manner that conserves, protects, and enhances its wildlife and other resources. The Secretary may only permit uses of the conservation area that are determined to further the primary purposes for which the conservation area was established, and may implement limits to visitation and use. Except in limited circumstances, motorized vehicles are permitted only on designated roads. Persons who violate the act or its implementing regulations are subject to a fine and/or imprisonment.
Clean Air Act (CAA) 42 U.S.C. §§7401 et seq.	See Appendix B for description of requirements.
Comprehensive Environmental Response, Compensation, and Liability Act (CERCLA) 42 U.S.C. §§9601 et seq.	CERCLA authorizes federal actions to respond to the release or substantial threat of a release of a hazardous substance into the environment, and of a pollutant or contaminant which may present an imminent and substantial endangerment to the public health or welfare. The act established liability of certain persons associated

Laws Waived	Pertinent Requirements
	with a release of hazardous substances for cleanup costs, natural resource damages, and the costs of federal public health studies. Federal departments, agencies, and instrumentalities are subject to the act to the same extent as nongovernmental entities, including for purposes of liability.
Endangered Species Act (ESA) 16 U.S.C. §§1531 et seq.	See Appendix B for description of requirements.
Farmland Protection Policy Act (FPPA) 7 U.S.C. §§4201 et seq.	The FPPA requires the Department of Agriculture, in cooperation with other federal entities, to develop criteria for identifying the effects of federal programs on the conversion of farmland to nonagricultural uses. Federal agencies are thereafter required to use these criteria to identify farmland that is converted by federal programs and take into account the adverse effects of such programs on the preservation of farmland. Agencies must consider alternative actions, as appropriate, that could lessen such adverse effects.
Federal Land Policy and Management Act (FLPMA) 43 U.S.C. §§1701 et seq.	The FLPMA primarily establishes guidelines for the management, protection, and use of federal public lands, as administered by the Secretary of the Interior through the Bureau of Land Management. The law provides for BLM lands to be managed on a multiple-use, sustained-yield basis. Provisions pertain to land use planning, acquisition, exchange, disposal, withdrawal, rights of way, range management, wilderness study, and advisory groups, among others. Some provisions also pertain to National Forest System lands.
Federal Water Pollution Control Act (Clean Water Act) 33 U.S.C. §§1251 et seq.	See Appendix B for description of requirements.
Fish and Wildlife Coordination Act (FWCA) 16 U.S.C. §§661 et seq.	The FWCA generally provides that whenever the waters of any stream or other body of water are proposed to be modified by a federal agency, the agency must first consult with the United States Fish and Wildlife Service, Department of the Interior, and the head of the agency exercising administration over the wildlife resources of the state where the construction will occur, with a view to the conservation of wildlife resources.
Historic Sites, Buildings, and Antiquities Act (HSBAA) 16 U.S.C. §§461 et seq. (Act repealed by P.L. 113-287, §7; similar provisions now codified	The HSBAA declares it the national policy to preserve historic sites, buildings, and objects of national significance. The Secretary of the Interior, through the National Park Service, is charged with implementing the policy of the HSBAA, including through the acquisition,

Appendix D. (Continued)

Laws Waived	Pertinent Requirements
in Title 54 of the U.S. Code)	maintenance, administration of historic sites.
Migratory Bird Treaty Act (MBTA) 16 U.S.C. §§703 et seq.	See Appendix B for description of requirements.
National Environmental Policy Act (NEPA) 42 U.S.C. §§4321 et seq.	See Appendix B for description of requirements.
National Historic Preservation Act (NHPA) 16 U.S.C. §§470 et seq. (Act repealed by P.L. 113-287, §7; similar provisions now codified in Title 54 of the U.S. Code)	See Appendix B for description of requirements.
Noise Control Act (NCA) 42 U.S.C. §§4901 et seq.	Pursuant to the NCA, the federal government has established standards for maximum sound levels generated from a variety of commercial products, railways, and interstate motor carriers.
Safe Drinking Water Act (SDWA) 42 U.S.C. §§300f et seq.	The Safe Drinking Water Act provides federal authority for the establishment of standards and treatment requirements for public water supplies, control of the underground injection of wastes, and protection of sources of drinking water. Federal agencies involved in certain activities that may contaminate drinking water are subject to all federal, state, and local requirements concerning the protection of water systems to the same extent as any person is subject to such requirements.
Solid Waste Disposal Act (SWDA), as amended by the Resource Conservation and Recovery Act (RCRA) 42 U.S.C. §§6901 et seq.	Through the SWDA, as amended by RCRA, entities that transport or generate hazardous waste are required to comply with regulations concerning the management of waste. Moreover, each federal agency engaged in any activity resulting, or which may result, in the disposal or management of solid waste or hazardous waste is subject to all federal, state, and local requirements concerning such waste to the same extent as any person is subject to such requirements.
Wild and Scenic Rivers Act 16 U.S.C. §§1281 et seq.	The Wild and Scenic Rivers Act establishes a National Wild and Scenic Rivers System (System) protecting rivers and adjacent lands with important scenic, recreational, geologic, fish and wildlife, historic, cultural, or other similar values. Components of the System are to be administered in a manner that preserves their free-flowing condition in order to protect water quality and to fulfill other national conservation purposes.

APPENDIX E. LEGAL REQUIREMENTS WAIVED BY DHS FOR THE CONSTRUCTION OF PHYSICAL BARRIERS AND ROADS IN HIDALGO COUNTY, TEXAS

Laws Waived	Pertinent Requirements
Administrative Procedure Act (APA) 5 U.S.C. §§551 et seq.	See Appendix B for description of requirements.
American Indian Religious Freedom Act (AIRFA) 42 U.S.C. §1996	AIRFA ensures American Indian groups access to religious sites by directing federal agencies to consult with American Indian spiritual leaders to determine appropriate procedures to protect access and other religious rights.
Antiquities Act 16 U.S.C. §§431 et seq. (Act repealed by P.L. 113-287, §7; similar provisions now codified in Title 54 of the U.S. Code)	See Appendix D for description of requirements.
Archaeological and Historic Preservation Act (AHPA) 16 U.S.C. §§469 et seq.	See Appendix D for description of requirements.
Archeological Resources Protection Act (ARPA) 16 U.S.C. §§470aa et seq.	See Appendix D for description of requirements.
Clean Air Act (CAA) 42 U.S.C. §§7401 et seq.	See Appendix B for description of requirements.
Coastal Zone Management Act (CZMA) 16 U.S.C. §§1451 et seq.	See Appendix B for description of requirements.
Comprehensive Environmental Response, Compensation, and Liability Act (CERCLA) 42 U.S.C. §§9601 et seq.	See Appendix D for description of requirements.
Eagle Protection Act 16 U.S.C. §§668 et seq.	The Eagle Protection Act provides for the protection of the bald eagle and the golden eagle by prohibiting the taking, possession, and commerce of such birds.
Endangered Species Act (ESA) 16 U.S.C. §§1531 et seq.	See Appendix B for description of requirements.

Appendix E. (Continued)

Laws Waived	Pertinent Requirements
Farmland Protection Policy Act (FPPA) 7 U.S.C. §§4201 et seq.	See Appendix D for description of requirements.
Federal Grant and Cooperative Agreement Act of 1977 31 U.S.C. §§6303-6305	The Federal Grant and Cooperative Agreement Act governs the use of various types of agreements. This act imposes standards mandating the use of procurement contracts, grants, and cooperative agreements in specific situations, while allowing the use of non-standard agreements in other situations.
Federal Land Policy and Management Act (FLPMA) 43 U.S.C. §§1701 et seq.	See Appendix D for description of requirements.
Federal Water Pollution Control Act (Clean Water Act) 33 U.S.C. §§1251 et seq.	See Appendix B for description of requirements.
Fish and Wildlife Act of 1956 16 U.S.C. §§742a et seq.	The Fish and Wildlife Act establishes a comprehensive national fish, shellfish, and wildlife resources policy. The law requires the Secretary of Interior to develop measures for "maximum sustainable production of fish," make economic studies of the industry and recommend measures to insure the stability of fisheries, take steps "required for the development, management, advancement, conservation and protection of the fisheries resources," and take steps "required for the development, management, advancement, conservation, and protection of fish and wildlife resources" through research, acquisition of land or water, development of existing facilities, and other means.
Fish and Wildlife Coordination Act (FWCA) 16 U.S.C. §§661 et seq.	See Appendix D for description of requirements.
Historic Sites, Buildings, and Antiquities Act (HSBAA) 16 U.S.C. §§461 et seq. (Act repealed by P.L. 113-287, §7; similar provisions now codified in Title 54 of the U.S. Code)	See Appendix D for description of requirements.
Migratory Bird Treaty Act (MBTA) 16 U.S.C. §§703 et seq.	See Appendix B for description of requirements.
National Environmental Policy Act (NEPA)	See Appendix B for description of requirements.

Laws Waived	Pertinent Requirements
42 U.S.C. §§4321 et seq.	
National Historic Preservation Act (NHPA) 16 U.S.C. §§470 et seq. (Act repealed by P.L. 113-287, §7; similar provisions now codified in Title 54 of the U.S. Code)	See Appendix B for description of requirements.
National Wildlife Refuge System Administration Act 16 U.S.C. §§668dd-668ee	See Appendix C for description of requirements.
Native American Graves Protection and Repatriation Act (NAGPRA) 25 U.S.C. §§3001 et seq.	NAGPRA requires federal agencies and other institutions receiving federal funding to return Native American cultural items and human remains to their respective people. If federal officials anticipate that activities on federal and tribal land might have an effect on American Indian burial, or their activities inadvertently discover such burials, they must consult with American Indian tribal officials as part of their compliance duties.
Noise Control Act (NCA) 42 U.S.C. §§4901 et seq.	See Appendix D for description of requirements.
Religious Freedom Restoration Act (RFRA) 42 U.S.C. §2000bb	RFRA generally provides that the government may not substantially burden a person's exercise of religion, except when the government demonstratives that the action is in furtherance of a compelling government interest and is the least restrictive means of furthering that interest.
Rivers and Harbors Act of 1899 33 U.S.C. §403	The Rivers and Harbors Act prohibits the obstruction of navigable waters of the United States, or to excavate, fill, or alter the course, condition, or capacity of any port, harbor, channel, or other area within the reach of the act, unless a permit from the Army Corps of Engineers is obtained.
Safe Drinking Water Act 42 U.S.C. §§300f et seq.	See Appendix D for description of requirements.
Solid Waste Disposal Act (SWDA), as amended by the Resource Conservation and Recovery Act (RCRA) 42 U.S.C. §§6901 et seq.	See Appendix D for description of requirements.

Appendix F. Legal Requirements Waived by DHS for the Construction of Physical Barriers and Roads at Various Project Areas Located in California, Arizona, New Mexico, and Texas

Laws Waived	Pertinent Requirements
Administrative Procedure Act (APA) 5 U.S.C. §§551 et seq.	See Appendix B for description of requirements.
American Indian Religious Freedom Act (AIRFA) 42 U.S.C. §1996	See Appendix E for description of requirements.
Antiquities Act 16 U.S.C. §§431 et seq. (Act repealed by P.L. 113-287, §7; similar provisions now codified in Title 54 of the U.S. Code)	See Appendix D for description of requirements.
Archaeological and Historic Preservation Act (AHPA) 16 U.S.C. §§469 et seq.	See Appendix D for description of requirements.
Archeological Resources Protection Act (ARPA) 16 U.S.C. §§470aa et seq.	See Appendix D for description of requirements.
Arizona Desert Wilderness Act, Sections 301(a)-(f) P.L. 101-628	The waived sections of the Arizona Desert Wilderness Act designate certain lands in the Havasu National Wildlife Refuge, Imperial National Wildlife Refuge, Kofa National Wildlife Refuge, and Cabeza Prieta National Wildlife Refuge (all in Arizona) as components of the National Wilderness Preservation System to be administered under the Wilderness Act.
California Desert Protection Act, Sections 102(29) and 103, P.L. 103-433 Clean Air Act (CAA) 42 U.S.C. §§7401 et seq.	The waived provisions of the California Desert Protection Act designate certain lands managed by BLM as the Jacumba Wilderness, to be managed in accordance with the Wilderness Act. See Appendix B for description of requirements.
Coastal Zone Management Act (CZMA) 16 U.S.C. §§1451 et seq.	See Appendix B for description of requirements.
Comprehensive Environmental Response, Compensation, and Liability Act (CERCLA) 42 U.S.C. §§9601 et seq.	See Appendix D for description of requirements.

Laws Waived	Pertinent Requirements
Eagle Protection Act 16 U.S.C. §§668 et seq.	See Appendix E for description of requirements.
Endangered Species Act (ESA) 16 U.S.C. §§1531 et seq.	See Appendix B for description of requirements.
Farmland Protection Policy Act (FPPA) 7 U.S.C. §§4201 et seq.	See Appendix D for description of requirements.
Federal Land Policy and Management Act (FLPMA) 43 U.S.C. §§1701 et seq.	See Appendix D for description of requirements.
Federal Water Pollution Control Act (Clean Water Act) 33 U.S.C. §§1251 et seq.	See Appendix B for description of requirements.
Fish and Wildlife Act of 1956 16 U.S.C. §§742a et seq.	See Appendix E for description of requirements.
Fish and Wildlife Coordination Act (FWCA) 16 U.S.C. §§661 et seq.	See Appendix D for description of requirements.
Historic Sites, Buildings, and Antiquities Act (HSBAA) 16 U.S.C. §§461 et seq. (Act repealed by P.L. 113-287, §7; similar provisions now codified in Title 54 of the U.S. Code)	See Appendix D for description of requirements.
Migratory Bird Treaty Act (MBTA) 16 U.S.C. §§703 et seq.	See Appendix B for description of requirements.
Multiple Use and Sustained Yield Act of 1960 16 U.S.C. §§528-531	The Multiple Use and Sustained Yield Act declares that national forests are to be managed for outdoor recreation, range, timber, watershed, and fish and wildlife purposes, and in a way that provides a high level of resource outputs for perpetuity, but does not impair the productivity of the land.
National Environmental Policy Act (NEPA) 16 U.S.C. §§4321 et seq.	See Appendix B for description of requirements.
National Forest Management Act of 1976	The National Forest Management Act provides standards for the planning and management of the national forests by the Forest Service within the
16 U.S.C. §§1600 et seq. National Historic Preservation Act (NHPA) 16 U.S.C. §§470 et seq. (Act repealed by P.L.	Department of Agriculture. See Appendix B for description of requirements.

Appendix F. (Continued)

Laws Waived	Pertinent Requirements
113-287, §7; similar provisions now codified in Title 54 of the U.S. Code)	
National Park Service General Authorities Act 16 U.S.C. §§1a-1 et seq. (Act repealed by P.L. 113-287, §7; similar provisions now codified in Title 54 of the U.S. Code)	The National Park Service General Authorities Act is the organic statute for the National Park Service. The act calls for the preservation of certain lands and empowers the National Park Service to issue regulations and manage these lands.
National Park Service Organic Act 16 U.S.C. §§1, 2-4 (Act repealed by P.L. 113-287, §7; similar provisions now codified in Title 54 of the U.S. Code)	The National Park Service Organic Act calls for the preservation of certain lands and empowers the Secretary of the Interior to issue regulations and manage these lands. The Secretary of the Interior may make such regulations as necessary or proper for the use and management of parks, monuments, and reservations under the National Park Service's jurisdiction.
National Parks and Recreation Act of 1978, Sections 401(7), 403 and 404 P.L. 95-625	These sections of National Parks and Recreation Act designate a number of areas, including the Organ Pipe Cactus National Monument in Arizona as "wilderness" to be administered under the Wilderness Act.
National Wildlife Refuge System Administration Act 16 U.S.C. §§668dd-668ee	See Appendix C for description of requirements.
Native American Graves Protection and Repatriation Act (NAGPRA) 25 U.S.C. §§3001 et seq.	See Appendix E for description of requirements.
Noise Control Act (NCA) 42 U.S.C. §§4901 et seq.	See Appendix D for description of requirements.
Otay Mountain Wilderness Act of 1999 P.L. 106-145	The Otay Mountain Wilderness Act designates certain public lands in California as "wilderness" to be managed in accordance with the Wilderness Act. Any lands acquired by the United States within the designated area shall become part of the designated "wilderness area," and shall also be managed in accordance with the Wilderness Act.
Religious Freedom Restoration Act (RFRA) 42 U.S.C. §2000bb	See Appendix E for description of requirements.
Rivers and Harbors Act of 1899 33 U.S.C. §403	See Appendix E for description of requirements.

Laws Waived	Pertinent Requirements
Safe Drinking Water Act 42 U.S.C. §§300f et seq.	See Appendix B for description of requirements.
Solid Waste Disposal Act (SWDA), as amended by the Resource Conservation and Recovery Act (RCRA) 42 U.S.C. §§6901 et seq.	See Appendix D for description of requirements.
Wild and Scenic Rivers Act 16 U.S.C. §1281 et seq.	See Appendix D for description of requirements.
Wilderness Act 16 U.S.C. §§1131 et seq.	See Appendix C for description of requirements.

End Notes

[1] Illegal Immigration Reform and Immigrant Responsibility Act (IIRIRA), P.L. 104-208, div. C, §102(a)-(c), as amended by the REAL ID Act of 2005, P.L. 109-13, div. B, §102; the Secure Fence Act of 2006, P.L. 109-367, §3; and the Consolidated Appropriations Act, 2008 P.L. 110-161, div. E, §564(a). These requirements are codified at 8 U.S.C. §1103 note. Unless otherwise indicated in this report, references in footnote citations to "IIRIRA §102" refer to the current version of the statute. The text of the current version of IIRIRA §102 can be found at Appendix A.

[2] The U.S.-Mexico land border is approximately 1,933 miles. The U.S. border area includes California, Arizona, New Mexico, and Texas. For further information, see CRS Report RS21729, U.S. International Borders: Brief Facts, available upon request.

[3] IIRIRA §102(b).

[4] U.S. Customs and Border Protection (CBP) within DHS is the primary agency responsible for border security activities at U.S. land borders and ports of entry. Within CBP, the U.S. Border Patrol serves the lead role in border enforcement matters between ports of entry.

[5] Illegal Immigration Reform and Immigrant Responsibility Act (IIRIRA), P.L. 104-208, div. C, §102(a)-(c).

[6] See supra footnote 1 (providing citations to provisions amending IIRIRA).

[7] For a graphic illustration of these changes, see CRS Report R42138, Border Security: Immigration Enforcement Between Ports of Entry, by Lisa Seghetti, at "Figure 4. Tactical Infrastructure Appropriations and Miles of Border Fencing, FY1996-FY2013."

[8] DHS's use of the term "vehicle fence" to describe permanent vehicle barriers installed along the border appears to be of relatively recent vintage. Compare HOUSE COMMITTEE ON APPROPRIATIONS, DEPARTMENT OF HOMELAND SECURITY APPROPRIATIONS FOR FY2007, PT. IV, COMMITTEE PRINT, April 6, 2006 (statement by DHS Secretary Michael Chertoff describing DHS plans to construct "an additional 40 miles of pedestrian fence and 140 miles of vehicle barriers") with DHS Secretary Jeh Johnson, "Border Security in the 21st Century," Remarks as Delivered and Accompanying Slide Presentation; Oct. 9, 2014, available at http://www.dhs.gov/news/2014/10/09/remarks-secretary-homeland-securityjeh-johnson-border-security-21st-century (discussing DHS's construction of "vehicle fencing" from FY2000 through FY2013). DHS's usage of the term "vehicle

fencing" to describe types of permanent vehicle barriers being installed along the border appears to go back at least since October 2007, when DHS announced plans to construct 300 miles of "vehicle fence" along the southwest border as part of the Vehicle Fence 300 (VF-300) initiative.

[9] For discussion of policy considerations which may inform decisions as to whether to deploy fencing and other barriers along the border, see archived CRS Report RL33659, Border Security: Barriers Along the U.S. International Border, by former CRS policy analyst Marc R. Rosenblum and Michael John Garcia, at 26-34.

[10] See generally CRS Report R42138, supra footnote 7.

[11] See Remarks of DHS Secretary Jeh Johnson, supra footnote 8. Maps that roughly indicate the stretches of the U.S.- Mexico border where fencing was deployed as of June 2011 can be viewed at http://nemo.cbp.gov/borderpatrol/ 2435_southwest.pdf (last accessed on Apr. 2, 2015).

[12] See "The Border Security, Economic Opportunity, and Immigration Modernization Act, S.744: Hearing Before the Senate Committee on the Judiciary," Apr. 23, 2013 (remarks by DHS Secretary Janet Napolitano in response to question, stating that the U.S. Border Patrol had identified 653 miles along the southwest border where fencing was appropriate), transcript available at http://www.c-span.org/video/?312302-1/dhs-sec-napolitano-testifies-immigrationreform.

[13] IIRIRA §102(b)(1)(A). In identifying its proximity to achieving this 700-mile mandate, DHS has typically counted only primary pedestrian and vehicle fencing, rather than any secondary fencing that may have been constructed behind such fencing. See, e.g., DHS: THE PATH FORWARD, HEARING BEFORE THE HOUSE COMMITTEE ON HOMELAND SECURITY, SERIAL NO. 111-1, 111th Cong., 1st Sess. (2009), Written Responses by DHS Secretary Janet Napolitano to Questions Posed by Rep. Lamar Smith, at 65 (describing DHS as having "completed 611 miles of fence along the southwest border—301 miles of vehicle fence and 310 miles of primary pedestrian fence"). Indeed, the relevant statutory obligation refers to mileage along the southwest border where fencing is to be constructed, rather than the total mileage of fencing deployed by DHS along the border. See infra at "Miles Along the Border vs. Total Miles of Fencing."

[14] Compare S.REPT. 113-40, at 7 (2013) (report of Senate Judiciary Committee on version of S. 744, the Border Security, Economic Opportunity, and Immigration Act, reported out of Committee, 113th Cong., 1st Sess., describing DHS as "having 651 miles of fencing out of nearly 652 miles mandated by Congress"); S.REPT. 113-40, at 44 (report of Senate Appropriations Committee on homeland security appropriations legislation for FY2014 reported out of Committee, describing funds appropriated over the years as having "been used to construct the 651 miles of fencing and border infrastructure mandated by the Secure Fence Act, as amended"); with H.R. 2892, §560 111th Cong., 1st Sess. (2009) (as passed by Senate with engrossed amendment, amending IIRIRA §102 to impose additional specifications and deadlines "to meet the 700-mile fence requirement" of the section).

[15] United States v. Arizona, No. 2:10-cv-01413-SRB, Order Dismissing Arizona's Counterclaims (D. Az., Oct. 21, 2011).

[16] See, e.g., H.R. 399, 114th Cong., 1st Sess. (2015) (legislation reported by House Homeland Security Committee); S. 208, 114th Cong., 1st Sess. (2015); H.R. 4962, 113th Cong., 2nd Sess. (2014).

[17] Id. at §3(c)(1). The bill specifies 48 miles along the border where double-layered pedestrian fencing would be required to be installed. If such fencing were installed, it would result in

fencing having been deployed along a total of slightly more than 700 miles of the southwest border.

[18] Border construction activities had been previously authorized primarily for purposes such as boundary demarcation. For example, Congress had earlier authorized the executive branch "to construct and maintain fences, monuments and other demarcations of the boundary line between the United States and Mexico," in accordance with relevant boundary and water allocation treaties between the two countries. Act of August 19, 1935, 49 Stat. 660. Such authority was sometimes used to assist in immigration controls. See also S. REPT. 81-848, at 2 (discussing funds provided through FY1949 for the construction of ranch-type and chain-link fencing, as an aid to the Department of Agriculture, Immigration and Naturalization Service, and the Bureau of Customs "in maintaining their controls of the border and as an aid to demarking the boundary line"). Indeed, in the years immediately after World War II, legislative proposals were considered to fund two large-scale fencing projects proposed by the International Boundary and Water Commission (the international body responsible for overseeing implementation of the water and boundary treaties between the United States and Mexico). Together, these projects would have potentially covered over 1,000 miles of the southwest border with fencing. Some supporters of funding that projects suggested that, in addition to providing assistance in boundary demarcation, the proposed fencing could deter the illegal border crossings by aliens and smugglers, and also prevent the spread of disease from domesticated animals that grazed along the U.S.-Mexico border. Ultimately, however, Congress opted not to act on these proposals. For background, see S. REP.. 80-470 (1947) (report accompanying S.J. Res. 46, 80th Cong., 1st Sess., describing fencing projects that had been proposed by International Boundary and Water Commission and discussing potential benefits of funding the proposal); S. REP. 83-2227 (1954) (report accompanying S.114, 83rd Cong., 2nd Sess., discussing the scaling back of the International Boundary and Water Commission fencing proposal, and including written statements from executive officials opining that benefits of the fencing proposal did not warrant the expenditures necessary to complete the project).

[19] For several decades, the authority to interpret, implement, and enforce the immigration law was primarily vested with the Attorney General. The Attorney General, in turn, delegated authority over immigration enforcement and service functions to the Department of Justice's Immigration and Naturalization Service (INS), within which the U.S. Border Patrol was located. Following the establishment of DHS, pursuant to the Homeland Security Act of 2002 (P.L. 107- 296), the INS was abolished and its enforcement functions were generally transferred to DHS, along with Border Patrol. See 6 U.S.C. §251. IIRIRA §102 has been amended to specifically reference the DHS Secretary, rather than the Attorney General, as having responsibility for carrying out the construction of barriers along the border.

[20] Immigration and Nationality Act (INA), §103(a)(5), 8 U.S.C. §1103 (a)(5).

[21] For additional background, see CRS Report RS22026, Border Security: The San Diego Fence, by Marc R. Rosenblum and Michael John Garcia (citing fencing description contained in U.S. Government Accountability Office, Border Control—Revised Strategy Is Showing Some Positive Results, GAO/GGD-95-30, Jan.31, 1995), available upon request.

[22] P.L. 104-208, div. C., §102.

[23] IIRIRA§102, as amended, also includes provisions concerning the availability of judicial review of DHS waivers of legal requirements that constrain expeditious construction of fencing; the acquisition of easements on private land to construct fencing; and consultation

requirements with federal, state, tribal, and private entities regarding the placement of fencing.

[24] A federal statute's use of the word "shall" in reference to authorized agency action is often construed as imposing a mandatory obligation upon the agency to perform such action. See, e.g., Lopez v. Davis, 531 U.S. 230, 241 (2001) (describing statute's use of "shall" as imposing a "discretionless" obligation upon an agency, compared to the statute's separate use of "may" to provide permissive authority for agency action). However, the appropriate interpretation of "shall" in a provision ultimately depends upon the context. For additional discussion, see CRS Report 97-589, Statutory Interpretation: General Principles and Recent Trends, by Larry M. Eig.

[25] It seems unlikely that a court would find it had jurisdiction to consider a legal challenge as to the adequacy of DHS's implementation of IIRIRA Section 102(a). The Administrative Procedure Act (APA) authorizes a reviewing court to "compel agency action unlawfully withheld or unreasonably delayed," 5 U.S.C. §706(c), which the Supreme Court has construed to apply to "discrete agency action that [the agency] is required to take." Norton v. Southern Utah Wilderness Alliance (SUWA), 542 U.S. 55, 64 (2004) (italics in original). Writing for the unanimous Court in SUWA, Justice Scalia opined that the APA was not intended to enable "broad programmatic challenges" to the manner in which an agency carries out a statutory duty:

The principal purpose of the APA limitations we have discussed—and of the traditional limitations upon mandamus from which they were derived—is to protect agencies from undue judicial interference with their lawful discretion, and to avoid judicial entanglement in abstract policy disagreements which courts lack both expertise and information to resolve. If courts were empowered to enter general orders compelling compliance with broad statutory mandates, they would necessarily be empowered, as well, to determine whether compliance was achieved—which would mean that it would ultimately become the task of the supervising court, rather than the agency, to work out compliance with the broad statutory mandate, injecting the judge into day-to-day agency management... The prospect of pervasive oversight by federal courts over the manner and pace of agency compliance with such congressional directives is not contemplated by the APA.

Id. at 66-67. See also United States v. Arizona, No. 2:10-cv-01413-SRB, Order Dismissing Arizona's Counterclaims, at *16 (D. Az., Oct. 21, 2011) ("While the construction of the fencing and infrastructure improvements may be phrased in mandatory language, the IIRIRA...leaves the Secretary and the DHS with a great deal of discretion in deciding how, when, and where to complete the construction. Moreover, [IIRIRA does] not mandate any discrete agency action with the clarity to support a judicial order compelling agency action.") (internal citations omitted).

[26] SUWA, 542 U.S. at 64 (APA claim to judicially compel agency action, on the ground that such action had been unlawfully withheld or unreasonably delayed by the agency, "can proceed only where a plaintiff asserts that an agency failed to take a discrete agency action that it is required to take.").

[27] See Save Our Heritage Organization v. Gonzales, 533 F.Supp.2d 58, 61 (D.D.C. 2008) (distinguishing the Secretary's "general authority" to install barriers under IIRIRA Section 102(a) from the specific mandate under IIRIRA Section 102(b) to construct fencing in certain areas).

[28] IIRIRA §102(b)(1)(A) ("In carrying out subsection (a), the Secretary of Homeland Security shall construct reinforced fencing along not less than 700 miles of the southwest border.... ").

[29] United States v. 1.16 Acres of Land, More or Less, Situate in Cameron County, Tex., 585 F.Supp.2d 901, 907 (S.D. Tex. 2008) (relying on dictionary definition of "vicinity" to interpret IIRIRA provision authorizing acquisition of lands "adjacent to or in the vicinity of an international land border when ... essential to control and guard the boundaries and borders of the United States").

[30] Regulations concerning the admission of non-citizens for purposes of transit to or from the United Nations Headquarters District generally provide that such persons remain "in immediate vicinity" of the District, which "is that area lying within a twenty-five mile radius of Columbus Circle, New York, NY." 8 C.F.R. §214.2(c)(2). Regulations specifying the distance which holders of border crossing cards—a form of documentation that may be issued to eligible Mexican citizens, enabling the holders to briefly travel to and from the United States without having to be multiple arrival/departure records by CBP—generally apply to travel within 25 miles from the border, though exceptions have been made authorizing travel of 75 miles within Arizona and 55 miles in New Mexico. 8 C.F.R. §235.1(h).

[31] United States v. Martinez-Fuerte, 428 U.S. 543, 555 (1976) (characterizing a prior Supreme Court decision concerning the permissibility of a warrantless search of an automobile 25 air miles from the U.S.-Mexico border, Almeida v. Sanchez, 413 U.S. 266 (1973), as involving a search occurring "in the general vicinity of the border").

[32] Arguably, provisions in federal immigration law and other federal statutes may be relevant in assessing what may permissibly be deemed "the vicinity of the United States border" for purposes of IIRIRA Section 102. The Immigration and Nationality Act authorizes immigration enforcement officers to engage in warrantless searches of vessels and vehicles within a "reasonable distance" from the border for purposes of detecting illegal entrants. Immigration and Nationality Act (INA) §287(a)(3); 8 U.S.C. §1357(a)(3). The term "reasonable distance" has long been interpreted under regulation to potentially cover distances up to 100 miles from the border. 8 C.F.R. §287.1(a)(2). The INA also expressly provides that immigration officers may permissibly access private lands to detect unlawfully present aliens, provided that such lands are located "within a distance of twenty-five miles" from the boundaries of the United States. Id.

[33] P.L. 104-208, div. C, §102(b). As originally enacted, IIRIRA Section 102(b) also provided authority for the acquisition of necessary easements to facilitate fence construction, required that certain safety features be incorporated into the design of the fence, and authorized an appropriation not to exceed $12 million. The current version of IIRIRA has relocated the provisions concerning easements and safety features, and has revised the appropriations authorization to cover "such sums as may be necessary to carry out" the requirements of Section 102(b). See IIRIRA (as amended), §102(b)(2)-(4).

[34] See CRS Report RS22026, Border Security: The San Diego Fence, by Marc R. Rosenblum and Michael John Garcia.

In late 2003, the California Coastal Commission (CCC) essentially halted further construction of the San Diego Fence. The CCC determined that CBP had not demonstrated, among other things, that the project was "to the maximum extent practicable" consistent with the policies of the California Coastal Management Program—a state program approved under the federal Coastal Zone Management Act, 16 U.S.C. §§1451, et seq. See California Coastal Commission, W 13a Staff Report and Recommendation on Consistency Determination, CD-063-03, Oct. 2003, available at http://www.coastal.ca.gov/cd/W8a-10-2003.pdf [hereinafter "CCC Report"]. According to the CCC Report, neither the CCC nor federal immigration authorities construed IIRIRA as mandating the construction of second and third layers of fencing along the entirety of the 14-mile fencing project, though the CCC Report does not discuss the reasons why this conclusion had been reached. Id. at 4 n.1.

[35] See infra at "Authority to Waive Legal Requirements Impeding Construction of Roads and Barriers."

[36] Dept. of Homeland Security, "Determination Pursuant to Section 102 of the Illegal Immigration Reform and Immigrant Responsibility Act of 1996 as Amended by Section 102 of the REAL ID Act of 2005," 70 FED. REG. 55622- 02 (2005) (waiving certain legal requirements to facilitate completion of San Diego fence project). Legislation has been introduced in the 114th Congress to compel improvements or modifications to current fencing in San Diego and other border areas. See H.R. 399, Secure Our Borders First Act of 2015, 114th Cong., 1st Sess. (as reported by the House Homeland Security Committee) (requiring replacement of certain fencing in San Diego border sector, along with construction of seven additional miles of double-layered fencing in the border sector).

[37] DHS could apparently still deploy additional fencing layers in the San Diego region pursuant to the general authority conferred to it under IIRIRA Section 102, if the agency deemed further fencing to be appropriate. Save Our Heritage Org., 533 F. Supp. 2d at 61 (although IIRIRA Section 102(b) was amended to remove earlier requirement that DHS construct fencing along the border near San Diego, DHS could still complete the fencing project pursuant to the general authority conferred by IIRIRA Section 102(a)).

[38] The Secure Fence Act also instructed the DHS Secretary, within 18 months, to "take all actions [he] determines necessary and appropriate to achieve and maintain operational control over the entire international land and maritime border," and provide Congress with annual reports on "progress made in achieving and maintaining operational control." P.L. 109-367, §2. "Operational control" is defined as "the prevention of all unlawful entries into the United States, including entries by terrorists, other unlawful aliens, instruments of terrorism, narcotics, and other contraband." DHS has construed this mandate as not requiring that the agency have actually obtained operational control of the borders within 18 months of the Secure Fence Act's enactment. Rather, the executive branch has interpreted the act as requiring DHS to have, within 18 months of enactment, taken all steps it determined necessary to achieve operational control, and keep Congress regularly informed of the steps it was taking through the submission of annual reports. See United States v. Arizona, No. 2:10-cv-01413-SRB, Counterdefendants' Reply in Support of Motion to Dismiss Counterclaims, at 5-6 (D. Az., Jul. 12, 2011). See also Department of Homeland Security Appropriations Act, 2010, P.L. 111-83, 123 Stat. 2142, 2146 (requiring, as a condition to the obligation of certain funds, that the DHS Secretary provide a report on the "progress made... in terms of obtaining operational control of the entire border of the United States). A legal challenge by the State of Arizona, which alleged that DHS had failed to comply with the requirements of the Secure Fence Act, was dismissed on jurisdictional grounds, as the reviewing district court found that the act's requirement concerning "operational control" did not mandate a discrete action that the court could compel. United States v. Arizona, No. 2:10-cv-01413-SRB, Order Dismissing Arizona's Counterclaims, at 15. (D. Az., Oct. 21, 2011).

[39] Secure Fence Act, P.L. 109-367, §3. The act mandated fencing:

(i) extending from 10 miles west of the Tecate, California, port of entry to 10 miles east of the Tecate, California, port of entry;

(ii) extending from 10 miles west of the Calexico, California, port of entry to 5 miles east of the Douglas, Arizona, port of entry;

(iii) extending from 5 miles west of the Columbus, New Mexico, port of entry to 10 miles east of El Paso, Texas;

(iv) extending from 5 miles northwest of the Del Rio, Texas, port of entry to 5 miles southeast of the Eagle Pass, Texas, port of entry; and

(v) extending 15 miles northwest of the Laredo, Texas, port of entry to the Brownsville, Texas, port of entry.

[40] 153 CONG. REC. 9890 (2007)(statement by Sen. Jeff Sessions, observing that DHS had found that, because of topographical issues along the border, the Secure Fence Act effectively required deployment of fencing along "close to 854 topographical miles").

[41] Secure Fence Act, P.L. 109-367, §3.

[42] Id.

[43] Id.

[44] IIRIRA §102(b)(1)(A).

[45] IIRIRA §102(b)(1)(D).

[46] Secure Fence Act, P.L. 109-367, §3.

[47] IIRIRA §102(b)(1)(B).

[48] IIRIRA §102(c)(i). The Consolidated Appropriations Act further provided that funds appropriated for FY2008 could not be expended for border construction activities under IIRIRA Section 102, unless DHS satisfied this consultation requirement. P.L. 110-161, div. E, §564(b).

[49] IIRIRA §102(c)(ii).

[50] See HOUSE COMMITTEE ON APPROPRIATIONS, COMMITTEE PRINT ON CONSOLIDATED APPROPRIATIONS ACT, 2008, 110th Cong., 2nd Sess. (2008).

[51] S.Amdt. 2412, offered as an amendment to S.Amdt. 2383, proposed by Sen. Robert Byrd in the nature of a substitute to H.R. 2638, Department of Homeland Security Appropriations Act, 2008, 110th Cong., 1st Sess.

[52] See 153 CONG. REC. S9948-9961 (daily ed., Jul 25, 2007) (reprinting text of amendment).

[53] See id. at 9871 (statement by Sen. Graham that, "The goal of this amendment is to provide complete operational control of the U.S.-Mexican border. It will...[among other things]...allow us to appropriate...300 miles of vehicle barriers...[and] 700 miles of border fencing."), and 9878 (statement by Sen. Sessions describing the amendment as ensuring the funding of 700 miles of border fencing).

[54] Id. at 9891 (statement by Sen. Cornyn). With respect to DHS decisions regarding the location of fencing, Sen. Cornyn stated:

Coming from a border State with 1,600 miles of common border with Mexico, this is a personal issue to many of my constituents, particularly. While some, such as [fellow amendment co-sponsor Sen. Sessions], believe strongly in the need for more fencing along the border, it is controversial along the border in south Texas....I noticed most of the property abutting the Rio Grande River is private property. I am not sure the Border Patrol or the Department of Homeland Security has really thought through the fencing idea and what it would mean to condemn through eminent domain proceedings private property along the border in Texas. I am informed that in Arizona and other places, much of the property along the border is already owned by the Federal Government, so we don't have that issue. But I have found in Texas, this is a controversial issue. I have been pleased to work with my colleague, Senator Hutchison, to make sure that in this amendment and in every opportunity, we have insisted upon consultation with local elected officials and property owners to achieve the most effective means of border security, recognizing that result is nonnegotiable but how we get there should be the subject of consultation and negotiation.

Id.

[55] See id. at 9895-9897 (concerning deliberations on decision to rule amendment out of order). The Senate voted to sustain the decision of the chair by a vote of 52-44.

[56] S.Amdt. 2480, offered as an amendment to S.Amdt. 2383, proposed in the nature of a substitute to H.R. 2638, Department of Homeland Security Appropriations Act, 2008, 110th Cong., 1st Sess.

[57] See 153 CONG. REC. S10059 (daily ed., Jul 26, 2007) (reprinting text of amendment).

[58] Id. at S10061.

[59] S.Amdt. 2486, offered as an amendment to S.Amdt. 2383, proposed in the nature of a substitute to H.R. 2638, Department of Homeland Security Appropriations Act, 2008, 110th Cong., 1st Sess. The text of the amendment is reprinted in 153 CONG. REC. S10102-10103 (daily ed., Jul. 26, 2007).

[60] Whereas the original Graham amendment would have required the deployment of fencing along 370 miles of the southwest border by the end of 2008, the revised amendment introduced by Sen. Hutchison called for 370 miles "or other mileage identified" by the Secretary of Homeland Security to be constructed in that period. The Hutchison amendment also did not include the earlier amendment's requirement that DHS complete a triple-layered fence near San Diego.

[61] Id. at S10103.

[62] Id. at S10059.

[63] H.R. 2638, Department of Homeland Security Appropriations Act, 2008, 110th Cong., 1st Sess. (passed by Senate with engrossed amendment).

[64] For further discussion of the process by which the omnibus was enacted can be found in CRS Report RL34298, Consolidated Appropriations Act for FY2008: Brief Overview, by Robert Keith.

[65] Consolidated Appropriations Act, 2008 P.L. 110-161, div. E, §564(a).

[66] Explanatory materials produced for the enacted Appropriations Act do not address why the Hutchison amendment was included in the final version of the act, but not the Graham amendment. See HOUSE APPROPRIATIONS COMMITTEE PRINT ON 2008 APPROPRIATIONS ACT, supra footnote 50.

[67] See Save Our Heritage Organization, 533 F.Supp.2d at 61 (upholding authority of DHS to construct additional double-layered fencing along border near San Diego under IIRIRA Section 102(a)).

[68] See, e.g., HEARING BEFORE THE HOUSE HOMELAND SECURITY COMMITTEE: THE CHALLENGE OF ALIGNING PROGRAMS, PERSONNEL, AND RESOURCES TO ACHIEVE BORDER SECURITY, SERIAL NO. 110-129, 110th Cong., 2nd Sess., Prepared Statement of DHS Secretary Chertoff (distinguishing between pedestrian and vehicle fencing, but counting both types in discussing DHS efforts to satisfy IIRIRA Section 102(b)'s fencing requirements); HOUSE COMMITTEE ON HOMELAND SECURITY, DEPARTMENT OF HOMELAND SECURITY APPROPRIATIONS FOR 2010, PART 1A, COMMITTEE PRINT (2010), CBP Budget Request and Supporting Information, at 667 ("As of April 4, 2009 ... CBP has constructed fencing totaling 618.6 miles along the southwest border (316.6 miles of pedestrian and 302 miles of vehicle fence) and contracts for all fencing projects needed to complete the approximately 670 miles of pedestrian or vehicle fence have been awarded."). HOUSE COMMITTEE ON HOMELAND SECURITY, DEPARTMENT OF HOMELAND SECURITY APPROPRIA-

TIONS FOR FY2011, PART 1A, COMMITTEE PRINT (2011), CBP Budget Justification for FY2011, at 781 ("As of January 1, 2010, CBP has constructed fencing totaling 642.8 miles along the southwest border (344.3 miles of pedestrian and 298.5 miles of vehicle fence).").

[69] Vehicle fencing is "used primarily in remote areas to prohibit vehicles engaged in drug trafficking and alien smuggling operations from crossing the border." Government Accountability Office (GAO), Secure Border Initiative Fence Construction Costs, Jan. 9, 2009, at 2.

[70] See, e.g., 155 CONG. REC. S7227-S7228 (daily ed., Jul. 8, 2009) (statement by Sen. James DeMint in support of amendment, approved by Senate by ultimately not enacted, requiring fencing under IIRIRA Section 102(b) to be pedestrian fencing).

[71] "Reinforced fencing" is not defined by statute, but is commonly used to refer to fencing which is constructed in a manner that makes it more durable and sturdy than a typical fence.

[72] Photos of various types of fencing that have been deployed by DHS along the southwest border can be viewed at http://nemo.cbp.gov/borderpatrol/2435_southwest.pdf (identifying locations of installed fencing as of June 2011).

[73] While IIRIRA Section 102(b) seems to distinguish "fencing" from other types of "physical barriers," it does not specify any particular features that deployed fencing must have, beyond being reinforced. Accordingly, at least so long as deployed barriers can reasonably be construed to constitute "fencing," as that term is ordinarily used, it seems that DHS would have considerable discretion to determine the appropriate type to be deployed at any particular location.

[74] See Written Responses by DHS Secretary Napolitano to Questions by House Homeland Security Committee, supra footnote 13, at 65 (identifying only primary pedestrian and vehicle fencing when identifying mileage of fencing deployed along southwest border pursuant to IIRIRA Section 102(b)).

[75] This second mandate also contemplates the construction of additional roads, barriers, and border infrastructure to achieve operational control, but these infrastructure requirements appear in a difference clause than the fencing requirement. The mileage requirement contained in IIRIRA Section 102(b) appears to apply only to fencing, and not to other infrastructure described in the subsection.

[76] See, e.g., HEARING BEFORE THE HOUSE HOMELAND SECURITY COMMITTEE: THE CHALLENGE OF ALIGNING PROGRAMS, PERSONNEL, AND RESOURCES TO ACHIEVE BORDER SECURITY, SERIAL NO. 110-129, 110th Cong., 2nd Sess., Prepared Statement of DHS Secretary Chertoff ("We made a commitment to have in place a total of 670 miles of pedestrian and vehicle fencing—including 370 miles of pedestrian fence and 300 miles of vehicle fence-on the southern border by the end of this calendar year to disrupt the entry of illegal immigrants, drugs, and vehicles.").

[77] The Secretary's authority to identify "other mileage" for installation of priority fencing expired on December 31, 2008. IIRIRA §102(b)(1)(B)(i).

[78] A 2009 GAO Report states:

> In September 2008, DHS revised its goal of completing the full 670 miles of fencing by December 31, 2008. As an interim step, DHS committed to have 661 miles either built, under construction, or under contract by December 31, 2008, but did not set a goal for the number of miles it planned to complete by December 31, 2008. As of December 31, 2008, DHS had completed 578 miles of fencing, meeting the interim statutory goal to complete 370 miles of fencing by that time.

GAO, Secure Border Initiative: Technology Deployment Delays Persist and the Impact of Border Fencing Has Not Been Assessed, Sept. 9, 2009, at p.8.

[79] See Remarks of DHS Secretary Jeh Johnson, supra footnote 8 (describing amount of fencing deployed by October 2014).

[80] IIRIRA §102(b)(1)(D).

[81] Secure Fence Act, P.L. 109-367, §3. See also supra footnote 39 (reprinting text of Secure Fence Act provision identifying particular stretches of the border where double-layered fencing was required to be deployed).

[82] Id. at §102(b)(1)(A).

[83] See Webster v. Doe, 486 U.S. 592, 600 (1988) (describing statute, providing that CIA Director may terminate employment of personnel whenever the Director "deems such termination necessary or advisable in the interests of the United States," as "exud[ing] deference to the Director, and appears to us to foreclose the application of any meaningful judicial standard of review.").

[84] The provision is entitled a "Limitation on requirements."

[85] See, e.g., Cisneros v. Alpine Ridge Group, 508 U.S. 10, 19 (1993) ("As we have noted previously in construing statutes, the use of ... a 'notwithstanding' clause clearly signals the drafter's intention that the provisions of the "notwithstanding" section override conflicting provisions of any other section.").

[86] Hibbs v. Winn, 542 U.S. 88, 101 (2004) (quoting 2A N. SINGER, STATUTES AND STATUTORY CONSTRUCTION §46.06, (rev. 6th ed. 2000)).

[87] See supra at "Legislative History."

[88] 153 CONG. REC. S10059 (daily ed. Jul. 26, 2007) (adding Sen. Hutchinson as co-sponsor to Graham amendment to homeland security appropriations bill, approved same day as amendment to IIRIRA Section 102(b), requiring completion of 700 miles of fencing within two years).

[89] See Gilman v. Department of Homeland Security, 32 F.Supp.3d 1, 5 (D.D.C. 2014) (describing IIRIRA Section 102(b) as having been "amended to mandate 'reinforced fencing along not less than 700 miles of the southwest border' and [to charge] the Secretary of Homeland Security with completing ... reinforced fencing [in priority areas] by the end of 2008. The precise location of the fence, however, was left to ... [DHS] to determine 'where fencing would be most practical and effective.... '"); Arizona, No. 2:10-cv-01413-SRB, Order Dismissing Arizona's Counterclaims, at 16 (D. Az., Oct. 21, 2011) ("[A]s amended by the 2008 Appropriations Act, [IIRIRA Section 102(b)] provides for the construction of 700 miles of fencing and additional infrastructure along the border 'where [it] would be most practical and effective.'"); United States v. 1.04 Acres of Land, More or Less, Situate in Cameron County, Tex., 538 F.Supp.2d 995, 1004 (S.D. Tex. 2008) (describing the most recent amendments to IIRIRA Section 102(b) as "remov[ing] references to specific areas for the construction of the fence, giving the Secretary discretion on where to put the fencing. The Secretary of Homeland Security now has a general mandate to construct at least 700 miles of fencing along the United States-Mexico border where fencing would be most practical and effective."); See also United States v. 1.16 Acres of Land, More or Less, Situate in Cameron County, Tex., 585 F.Supp.2d 901, 907 n.3 (S.D. Tex. 2008) "[IIRIRA] Section 102(b) requires the Secretary of Homeland Security to construct a minimum number of miles of fencing in identified areas in the country.").

[90] Dept. of Homeland Security, "Determination Pursuant to Section 102 of the Illegal Immigration Reform and Immigrant Responsibility Act of 1996, as Amended," 73 FED. REG. 18294 (April 3, 2008), republished with additional document in 73 FED. REG. 19077

(April 8, 2008); "Determination Pursuant to Section 102 of the Illegal Immigration Reform and Immigrant Responsibility Act of 1996, as Amended," 73 FED. REG. 18293 (April 3, 2008), republished with additional document in 73 FED. REG. 19078 (April 8, 2008).

[91] Written Responses by DHS Secretary Napolitano to Questions by House Homeland Security Committee, supra footnote 13, at 65. Although Secretary Napolitano's written statement refers to DHS's obligation to complete "700 total miles of fence," rather than fencing along "700 miles of the border," it is not clear that this was a purposeful distinction. As previously noted, DHS has appeared to consistently count only primary pedestrian and vehicle fencing towards its efforts to fulfill the mandates of IIRIRA Section 102(b), rather than any secondary or tertiary fencing that may be deployed behind it. See id. (describing DHS as having "completed 611 miles of fence along the southwest border—301 miles of vehicle fence and 310 miles of primary pedestrian fence").

[92] See GAO Report, footnote 78, at p.8. HOUSE COMMITTEE ON APPROPRIATIONS, DEPARTMENT OF HOMELAND SECURITY APPROPRIATIONS FOR 2011, PT. 3, COMMITTEE PRINT, Written Responses by Chief David Aguilar, CBP Acting Deputy Commissioner, to Questions Posed by Rep. Sam Farr, at 210 ("To date, DHS has completed 645.8 miles of fencing out of nearly 652 planned miles, including 298.5 miles of vehicle barriers and 347.3 miles of pedestrian fence (the Border Patrol has determined after extensive study that only 652 miles—not 700 miles—of fencing is operationally necessary to secure the southwest border).").

[93] ProQuest Transcript, "Hearing Before Senate Committee on the Judiciary: Comprehensive Immigration Reform, Panel 1," Feb. 13, 2013. Secretary Napolitano responded to a question regarding fence deployment by stating, "On the fence, the original act was for 700 miles. There was a subsequent amendment or adjustment to that I think it was proposed by Senator Hutchison, to 655 miles. All but one mile of that is now complete [sic]. And the one mile are different little sections, most of them are in some litigation or other with private property owners."

[94] For more extensive discussion of this litigation, as well as other lawsuits brought by U.S. states which challenge federal immigration enforcement policies, see CRS Report R43839, State Challenges to Federal Enforcement of Immigration Law: Historical Precedents and Pending Litigation, by Kate M. Manuel.

[95] Arizona, No. 2:10-cv-01413-SRB, Counterdefendants' Reply in Support of Their Motion to Dismiss Counterclaims, at 9 (D. Az., Jul. 12, 2011) ("DHS has already completed 649 of the 700 miles—over 92% of the target that Congress set a little over three years ago without a deadline—and that much of this fencing covers the Arizona border."); Counterdefendants' Motion to Dismiss Counterclaims and Memorandum of Law in Support Thereof, at 22 (D. Az. Apr. 12, 2001) ("Section 102 of the IIRIRA (as amended) vests in the Secretary complete discretion for determining how to gain operational control of the border and where fencing and additional measures should be utilized in that effort... Further, the Act prescribes no deadline for completing the construction of 700 miles of fencing or installing additional physical barriers, roads, lighting, cameras, and sensors along the southwest border, despite the fact that the Act prescribed deadlines in other instances.").

[96] See, e.g., Chevron, U.S.A., Inc. v. Natural Resources Defense Council, Inc., 467 U.S. 837, 844 (1984) ("[A] court may not substitute its own construction of a statutory provision for a reasonable interpretation made by the administrator of an agency.").

[97] Id. at 842-843 ("If the intent of Congress is clear, that is the end of the matter; for the court, as well as the agency, must give effect to the unambiguously expressed intent of Congress. If, however, the court determines Congress has not directly addressed the precise question at

issue, the court does not simply impose its own construction on the statute, as would be necessary in the absence of an administrative interpretation. Rather, if the statute is silent or ambiguous with respect to the specific issue, the question for the court is whether the agency's answer is based on a permissible construction of the statute."); United States v. Shimer, 367 U.S. 374, 383 (1961) (When an agency is tasked with "accommodation of conflicting policies that were committed to the agency's care by the statute, we should not disturb it unless it appears from the statute or its legislative history that the accommodation is not one that Congress would have sanctioned.").

[98] In Chevron, U.S.A., Inc. v. Natural Resources Defense Council, Inc., 467 U.S. 837, 844 (1984), the Supreme Court recognized situations where Congress has expressly or impliedly delegated interpretative authority over a statute to an agency, a reviewing court will typically oblige to an agency's interpretation so long as it is not "arbitrary, capricious, or manifestly contrary to the statute." Id. at 844. Typically, a reviewing court will find an express or implied delegation of interpretive authority warranting Chevron deference in situations where there is "express congressional authorizations to engage in the process of rulemaking or adjudication that produces regulations or rulings for which deference is claimed." United States v. Mead Corp., 533 U.S. 218, 229-230 (2001). See also Christensen v. Harris County, 529 U.S. 576, 587 (2000 ("Interpretations such as those in opinion letters—like interpretations contained in policy statements, agency manuals, and enforcement guidelines, all of which lack the force of law—do not warrant Chevron-style deference.")

[99] Skidmore v. Swift & Co., 323 U.S. 134, 140 (1944). In some instances, the Supreme Court has recognized that "[a]n agency interpretation of a relevant provision which conflicts with the agency's earlier interpretation is entitled to considerably less deference than a consistently held agency view." INS v. Cardoza-Fonseca, 480 U.S. 421, 446, n.30 (1987) (internal quotations omitted). However, a change in agency interpretation is not itself a ground to view the later construction as impermissible, at least so long as reasons for the change in policy are adequately explained. See, e.g., National Cable & Telecommunications Ass'n v. Brand X Internet Services, 545 U.S. 967, 981 (2005) ("Agency inconsistency is not a basis for declining to analyze the agency's interpretation under the Chevron framework. Unexplained inconsistency is, at most, a reason for holding an interpretation to be an arbitrary and capricious change from agency practice under the Administrative Procedure Act. For if the agency adequately explains the reasons for a reversal of policy, change is not invalidating, since the whole point of Chevron is to leave the discretion provided by the ambiguities of a statute with the implementing agency.") (internal quotations and citations omitted).

[100] In NationsBank of North Carolina, N.A. v. Variable Annuity Life Ins. Co., 513 U.S. 251 (1996), the Supreme Court afforded Chevron deference to the Comptroller of Currency's "deliberative conclusions" regarding the interpretation of banking laws, on account of the Comptroller being "charged with the enforcement of banking laws to an extent that warrants the invocation" of a high standard of deference to his interpretations. Subsequently in United States. v. Mead Corp., the Supreme Court seemed to suggest that the conclusion it reached in NationsBank was at least partially on account of "longstanding precedent" recognizing the Comptroller's interpretative authority. Mead Corp., 533 U.S. at 231 n.13. Accordingly, the possible relevance of NationsBank to decisions outside the banking context, including with respect to DHS interpretations of fencing requirements of IIRIRA is unclear.

[101] Arizona, No. 2:10-cv-01413-SRB, Order Dismissing Arizona's Counterclaims, at 16 (D. Az., Oct. 21, 2011).

[102] Id.

[103] 5 U.S.C. §706(1).

[104] For further discussion, see CRS Report R43013, Administrative Agencies and Claims of Unreasonable Delay: Analysis of Court Treatment, by Daniel T. Shedd. See also Telecommunications Research and Action Center v. F.C.C., 750 F.2d 70. 79-80 (D.C. Cir. 1984) (observing that "the first stage of judicial inquiry is to consider whether the agency's delay is so egregious as to warrant mandamus," and identifying several factors that should be appropriately considered when assessing an agency delay claim). In situations where a statutory provision requiring agency action does not contain a statutory deadline for completion of such action, some reviewing courts considering APA-based challenges to the agency inaction will assess whether the action was "unreasonably delayed" rather than "unlawfully withheld." See Forest Guardians v. Babbitt, 174 F.3d 1178 (10th Cir. 1999).

[105] SUWA, 542 U.S. at 64. Even assuming that the deployment of fencing "along not less than 700 miles of the border where it would be most practical and effective" could be considered a discrete agency action that a court could compel, a court would unlikely be able to direct DHS to deploy such fencing at a specific location. See id. at 65 ("[W]hen an agency is compelled by law to act within a certain time period, but the manner of its action is left to the agency's discretion, a court can compel the agency to act, but has no power to specify what the action must be."); IIRIRA §102(b)(1)(D) (providing that DHS is not required to deploy fencing at "any particular location" when the DHS Secretary determines that other means are more appropriate for achieving operational control of that location).

[106] Arizona, No. 2:10-cv-01413-SRB, Order Dismissing Arizona's Counterclaims, at 16 (D. Az., Oct. 21, 2011) (in considering Arizona's motion seeking to compel completion of fencing, finding that IIRIRA, as amended, did "not mandate any discrete agency action with the clarity to support a judicial order compelling agency action," but not explaining reasoning for this conclusion).

[107] Lujan v. Defenders of Wildlife, 504 U.S. 555, 560-561 (1992).

[108] Arizona, No. 2:10-cv-01413-SRB, Order Dismissing Arizona's Counterclaims, at 4-5.

[109] P.L. 104-208, div. C, §102c. A general overview of relevant NEPA and ESA requirements in found in Appendix B.

[110] See CCC Report, supra footnote 34, at 10.

[111] For further discussion, see CRS Report RS22026, Border Security: The San Diego Fence, by Marc R. Rosenblum and Michael John Garcia, available upon request.

[112] See CCC Report, supra footnote 34, at 1-4.

[113] See H.REPT. 109-72, 109th Cong., 1st Sess. (2005) at 170-172 (conference report for emergency supplemental appropriations legislation to which the REAL ID Act was attached, describing purposes of the act).

[114] As initially introduced as H.R. 418, the REAL ID Act required the Secretary of DHS to waive "all laws" necessary to ensure expeditious construction of the security barriers. H.R. 418 was passed by the House as a stand-alone piece of legislation, but was subsequently attached as an amendment to House-passed H.R. 1268, the emergency supplemental appropriations bill for FY2005. During conference, language was revised in H.R. 1268, so that the Secretary was authorized, but not required, to waive "all legal requirements" deemed necessary to ensure construction of the security barriers. The conferees also added provisions to the REAL ID Act which made waiver decisions effective upon publication in the Federal Register and permitted federal court review of waiver decisions only in limited

circumstances. See H.REPT. 109-72, 109th Cong., 1st Sess. (2005) at 170-172 The conference version of H.R. 1268 was enacted on May 11, 2005.

[115] IIRIRA §102(c)(1).

[116] See David J. Barron and Todd D. Rakoff, In Defense of Big Waiver, 113 COLUM. L. REV. 265, 290 (2013) (examining history of broad statutory waivers, and observing that "As a matter of its formal reach...[the REAL ID Act] waiver may be the biggest Congress has yet passed.").

[117] See, e.g., Kate R. Bowers, Saying what the Law Isn't: Legislative Delegations of Waiver Authority in Environmental Laws, 34 HARV. ENVTL. L. REV. 257 (2010) (criticizing REAL ID Act's waiver expansion on policy grounds and on ground that it may represent a constitutionally impermissible delegation of legislative authority and result in the usurpation of judicial authority by the Executive); David J. Barron and Todd D. Rakoff, supra footnote 116, at 289- 290, 337-339 (discussing modern usage of large-scale delegations of waiver authority to administrative agencies and generally defending their constitutionally, but expressing concern regarding the breadth of the REAL ID Act waiver).

[118] See, e.g., Williams v. Rhodes, 393 U.S. 23, 29 (1968) ("[T]he Constitution is filled with provisions that grant Congress or the States specific power to legislate in certain areas; these granted powers are always subject to the limitations that they may not be exercised in a way that violates other specific provisions of the Constitution."). Indeed, IIRIRA Section 102(c)(2)(A) expressly provides that federal district courts have jurisdiction to hear claims arising from border construction projects "alleging a violation of the Constitution of the United States."

[119] In exercising waiver authority under IIRIRA, the DHS Secretary appears to have construed it as applying to physical infrastructure projects built in connection with the construction of barriers and roads, such as radio towers. See, e.g., Dept. of Homeland Security, "Determination Pursuant to Section 102 of the Illegal Immigration Reform and Immigrant Responsibility Act of 1996, as Amended," 73 Fed. Reg. 19078 (Apr. 8, 2008) (waiving laws related to access, staging, and construction in the project area including "installation and upkeep of fences, roads, supporting elements, draining, erosion controls, safety features, surveillance, communication and detection equipment of all types, radar and radio towers and lighting").

[120] With respect to each of the fencing projects conducted between 2008 and 2011 in which the Secretary had exercised waiver authority, DHS's CBP prepared an environmental stewardship plan (ESP) concerning the potential environmental effects of the project. After a project was completed, CBP would prepare an environmental stewardship summary report (ESSR) "documenting the final 'footprint' of the sections built under the waiver to provide an "as built" summary for the public and regulatory agencies." CBP, Environmental Stewardship Plans (ESPs) Environmental Stewardship Summary Reports (ESSRs), available at http://www.cbp.gov/about/environmental-cultural-stewardship/ nepa-documents/esp-essr.(providing links to ESPs and ESSRs).

[121] Dept. of Homeland Security, "Determination Pursuant to Section 102 of the Illegal Immigration Reform and Immigrant Responsibility Act of 1996 as Amended by Section 102 of the REAL ID Act of 2005," 70 FED. REG. 55622- 02, Sept. 22, 2005.

[122] Dept. of Homeland Security, "Determination Pursuant to Section 102 of the Illegal Immigration Reform and Immigrant Responsibility Act of 1996 as Amended by Section 102 of the REAL ID Act of 2005 and as Amended by the Secure Fence Act of 2006," 72 FED. REG. 2535-01, Jan. 19, 2007.

[123] Defenders of Wildlife v. Bureau of Land Management, Case 1:07-cv-01801-ESH (D.D.C. 2007). Plaintiffs' request for a temporary restraining order can be viewed at http://www.defenders.org/resources/publications/programs_and_policy/in_the_courts/san_pedro_border_wall_tro_filing.pdf.

[124] A description of NEPA's requirements is found in Appendix B.

[125] Dept. of Homeland Security, "Determination Pursuant to Section 102 of the Illegal Immigration Reform and Immigrant Responsibility Act of 1996 as Amended by Section 102 of the REAL ID Act of 2005 and as Amended by the Secure Fence Act of 2006," 72 FED. REG. 60870-01, Oct. 26, 2007.

[126] Dept. of Homeland Security, "Determination Pursuant to Section 102 of the Illegal Immigration Reform and Immigrant Responsibility Act of 1996, as Amended," 73 FED. REG. 18294 (April 3, 2008), republished with additional document in 73 FED. REG. 19077 (April 8, 2008).

[127] Dept. of Homeland Security, "Determination Pursuant to Section 102 of the Illegal Immigration Reform and Immigrant Responsibility Act of 1996, as Amended," 73 FED. REG. 18293 (April 3, 2008), republished with additional document in 73 FED. REG. 19078 (April 8, 2008).

[128] County of El Paso v. Chertoff, No. EP-08-CA-196, 2008 WL 4372693 (W.D. Tex. Aug. 29, 2008); Save Our Heritage Organization v. Gonzalez, 533 F. Supp. 2d 58 (D.D.C. 2008); Defenders of Wildlife v. Chertoff, 527 F. Supp. 2d 119 (D.D.C. 2007); Sierra Club v. Ashcroft, No. 04-CV-272, 2005 U.S. Dist. LEXIS 44244 (S.D. Cal. Dec. 13, 2005).

[129] County of El Paso, No. EP-08-CA-196, (W.D. Tex. Aug. 29, 2008), cert. denied, 129 S. Ct. 2789 (2009); Defenders of Wildlife, 527 F. Supp. 2d 119 (D.D.C. 2007), cert. denied, 128 S. Ct. 2962 (2008).

[130] Illegal Immigration Reform and Immigrant Responsibility Act, P.L. 104-208, div. C, §102(a)-(c), as amended by the REAL ID Act of 2005, P.L. 109-13, div. B, §102; the Secure Fence Act of 2006, P.L. 109-367, §3, and the Consolidated Appropriations Act, 2008 P.L. 110-161, div. E, §564(a). These requirements are codified at 8 U.S.C. §1103 note.

INDEX

#

20th century, 3, 4
9/11, 6, 15, 17, 43, 58

A

abuse, 42
access, 88, 93, 103, 112
accommodation, 110
accounting, 38, 41, 43
acquisitions, 22
adjustment, 109
Administrative Procedure Act, 78, 86, 88, 89, 93, 96, 102, 110
administrative support, 18
advancement, 94
adverse effects, 91
agencies, 7, 13, 17, 18, 44, 50, 57, 81, 82, 86, 90, 91, 92, 93, 95, 102, 112
Air Force, 88
air quality, 86
alien smuggling, 107
American Civil Liberties Union, 38, 58
APA, 78, 86, 88, 89, 93, 96, 102, 111
appropriations, 2, 3, 4, 15, 16, 17, 19, 20, 37, 70, 71, 76, 85, 100, 103, 108, 111
Appropriations Act, 19, 51, 61, 62, 63, 64, 69, 70, 71, 72, 73, 74, 76, 99, 104, 105, 106, 108, 113
Appropriations Committee, 100
arrests, 6, 42, 52
ASI, 21
assessment, 21, 32, 82, 87
assets, 8, 15, 21, 22, 43, 54, 58
asylum, 49
Attorney General, 11, 65, 80, 85, 101
authorities, vii, 62, 64, 65, 66, 68, 80, 103
authority, 18, 62, 63, 65, 66, 68, 72, 78, 79, 80, 81, 82, 83, 84, 85, 92, 101, 102, 103, 104, 106, 107, 110, 112
avoidance, 87

B

bail, 8
banking, 110
barriers, vii, 6, 18, 19, 20, 41, 43, 61, 62, 63, 65, 66, 67, 68, 69, 71, 72, 74, 76, 79, 80, 81, 82, 83, 84, 85, 88, 99, 100, 101, 102, 105, 107, 109, 111, 112
Barron, David J., 112
base, 57, 111
benefits, 2, 4, 37, 41, 44, 48, 101
bilateral, 42
birds, 41, 93
border control, 3, 5, 9
border crossing, 27, 37, 39, 40, 63, 101, 103

border security, vii, 1, 2, 3, 7, 15, 17, 18, 26, 27, 30, 31, 32, 33, 34, 37, 43, 44, 46, 54, 55, 64, 69, 77, 99, 105
Bureau of Customs and Border Protection, 16, 20, 48
Bureau of Justice Statistics, 58
Bureau of Labor Statistics, 29
Bureau of Land Management, 88, 91, 113
business model, 49
businesses, 2

C

car accidents, 57
CBC, 58
CBP, vii, 1, 7, 9, 10, 11, 12, 13, 14, 15, 16, 17, 18, 20, 22, 24, 25, 32, 33, 36, 38, 39, 40, 42, 43, 46, 47, 48, 49, 50, 51, 52, 53, 54, 55, 56, 58, 59, 63, 65, 68, 99, 103, 106, 109, 112
CERCLA, 90, 93, 96
CFR, 86
chain of command, 7
challenges, 26, 27, 102, 111
Chevron deference, 110
children, 47, 52, 57
CIA, 108
cities, 38
citizens, 12, 43, 49, 103
civil rights, 41, 43
clarity, 102, 111
classes, 22
Clean Air Act, 86, 90, 93, 96
Clean Water Act, 87, 88, 91, 94, 97
cleanup, 90
clients, 29
Coast Guard, 13
coding, 33
commerce, 70, 85, 93
commercial, 41, 92
communication, 112
communities, 2, 4, 7, 27, 37, 41, 43, 85
community, 6, 40, 89
competitiveness, 42
compliance, 80, 86, 95, 102
computer, 21
conference, 56, 111
conformity, 86
Congress, 1, 3, 4, 6, 15, 17, 19, 30, 33, 42, 43, 44, 47, 48, 49, 52, 53, 54, 55, 61, 62, 63, 64, 65, 67, 69, 70, 72, 74, 76, 80, 82, 83, 100, 101, 104, 109, 110, 112
conservation, 88, 89, 90, 91, 92, 94
Consolidated Appropriations Act, 19, 51, 61, 62, 63, 64, 69, 99, 105, 106, 113
constituents, 105
Constitution, 80, 86, 112
construction, vii, 6, 19, 20, 41, 42, 61, 62, 63, 64, 65, 66, 67, 68, 69, 73, 74, 76, 77, 78, 79, 80, 81, 82, 83, 84, 85, 90, 91, 99, 101, 102, 103, 104, 105, 107, 108, 109, 110, 111, 112
Consumer Price Index, 29
contaminant, 90
control measures, 86
controversial, 105
conversations, 55
cooperation, 18, 59, 89, 91
cooperative agreements, 94
cost, 21, 59, 63
counterterrorism, 18
country of origin, 48
covering, 66
CPI, 29
crimes, 42
criminal activity, 38
criminal statutes, 71
criminality, 38
criticism, 21, 57
cultural items, 95
culture, 70, 84
Customs and Border Protection, vii, 1, 16, 17, 20, 24, 39, 47, 48, 50, 51, 63, 99
Customs Service, 16, 18, 20

D

damages, 90
danger, 90
data collection, 31

database, 21, 43, 47, 49, 52
deaths, 2, 37, 38, 39, 42, 56
defendants, 11, 42
demographic change, 36
demographic characteristics, 38
Department of Agriculture, 91, 97, 101
Department of Commerce, 4
Department of Defense, 18, 22, 52, 65
Department of Homeland Security, vii, 1, 8, 47, 48, 50, 53, 58, 61, 62, 104, 105, 106, 108
Department of Justice, 4, 9, 11, 32, 47, 50, 54, 58, 77, 101
Department of Labor, 4
Department of the Interior, 58, 91
destruction, 44, 87, 90
detection, 30, 44, 84, 112
detention, 8, 11, 42
deterrence, 1, 5, 6, 25, 28, 31, 35, 39, 43, 46, 53, 55
diminishing returns, 43
directives, 102
distress, 56
district courts, 80, 85, 112
DOJ, 9, 11, 16, 50
drinking water, 92
drug smuggling, 5
drug trafficking, 5, 107
drugs, 7, 46, 107

E

economic activity, 41
economic change, 4
economic competitiveness, 42
economic downturn, 2, 23, 29, 36
education, 38
emergency, 111
employment, 4, 37, 57, 108
employment opportunities, 4, 57
endangered, 41, 87
endangered species, 41, 87
enforcement, vii, 1, 2, 3, 4, 5, 6, 7, 8, 9, 10, 12, 13, 15, 17, 18, 22, 23, 27, 29, 30, 31, 32, 33, 34, 35, 36, 37, 38, 39, 40, 41, 42, 43, 44, 45, 46, 48, 49, 50, 53, 55, 57, 59, 62, 63, 71, 77, 99, 101, 103, 109, 110
engineering, 18
environment, 40, 41, 43, 70, 84, 87, 90
environmental effects, 87, 112
environmental impact, 37, 63, 87
environmental impact statement, 87
Environmental Protection Agency, 86
EPA, 80, 87
equipment, 18, 22, 112
erosion, 41, 112
evidence, 2, 37, 39, 40, 43
exclusion, 48, 49
executive branch, 82, 101, 104
exercise, 82, 95
expenditures, 50, 101
expertise, 102
exposure, 38, 56

F

families, 40
family members, 57
farmland, 91
FBI, 52
fear, 38, 49
federal agency, 86, 87, 90, 91, 92
Federal Bureau of Investigation, 38, 52
federal courts, 42, 64, 102
federal government, 92, 105
federal law, vii, 50, 62, 65, 80
Federal Register, 76, 80, 81, 82, 85, 86, 111
federalism, 82
fencing, 2, 5, 6, 8, 18, 19, 20, 36, 41, 42, 43, 51, 61, 62, 63, 64, 65, 66, 67, 68, 69, 70, 71, 72, 73, 74, 75, 76, 77, 78, 79, 80, 83, 84, 85, 99, 100, 101, 102, 104, 105, 106, 107, 108, 109, 110, 111, 112
fingerprints, 25
fiscal year, 10, 13, 19, 25, 26, 46, 50
fish, 88, 92, 94, 97
Fish and Wildlife Service, 87, 88, 91
fisheries, 94
flight, 22
force, 110

foreign-born population, 32
formation, 15
formula, 45
fraud, 38, 49
funding, 4, 15, 16, 17, 20, 42, 62, 63, 83, 95, 101, 105
funds, 20, 71, 100, 101, 104, 105

G

GAO, 6, 35, 48, 51, 52, 54, 55, 58, 74, 101, 107, 108, 109
General Accounting Office, 6
governments, 70, 84
grants, 83, 94
grazing, 88
Great Depression, 3
growth, 15, 30
growth rate, 30
guardian, 50
guidance, 31
guidelines, 91, 110
guilty, 11
Gulf of Mexico, 22

H

habitat, 87
hair, 71
hazardous substance(s), 90
hazardous waste, 92
health, 90
height, 72
history, 3, 11, 21, 47, 51, 62, 64, 67, 70, 76, 110, 112
homeland security, 70, 71, 76, 100, 108
Homeland Security Act, 47, 101
House, 6, 11, 47, 48, 49, 50, 51, 53, 54, 55, 62, 65, 71, 76, 100, 104, 107, 109, 111
human, 5, 8, 18, 29, 43, 44, 49, 57, 87, 95
human remains, 95
human right(s), 43, 57
hunting, 88

I

ICE, 8, 12, 13, 15, 52
ideal, 10
identification, 18
images, 21
immigrants, 5, 6, 55, 107
immigration, vii, 1, 2, 3, 4, 5, 6, 8, 9, 10, 11, 14, 15, 18, 20, 22, 27, 32, 37, 42, 43, 44, 47, 48, 49, 50, 53, 56, 64, 65, 66, 67, 68, 71, 77, 80, 101, 103, 109
Immigration Act, 47, 50, 100
Immigration and Customs Enforcement (ICE), 13, 15
Immigration and Nationality Act, 9, 47, 49, 71, 85, 101, 103
imports, 4
imprisonment, 90
improvements, 6, 78, 102, 104
inadmissible, 9, 48
individuals, 25, 30, 31
industry, 94
inflation, 19, 29, 30
information sharing, 42
infrastructure, 1, 2, 5, 6, 8, 15, 18, 19, 20, 41, 43, 63, 64, 69, 73, 75, 77, 78, 79, 82, 100, 102, 107, 108, 112
initiation, 25
injury, 79
INS, 4, 5, 6, 16, 19, 20, 51, 55, 59, 101, 110
inspections, 16, 20
institutions, 89, 95
integration, 7
intelligence, 7, 18
Intelligence Reform and Terrorism Prevention Act, 47, 51
interference, 102
investments, 2, 43, 44
issues, 2, 3, 4, 33, 43, 87, 105

J

Judiciary Committee, 11, 51, 77, 100
jurisdiction, 79, 80, 85, 89, 98, 102, 112

K

kill, 87

L

labor market(s), 57
landscape, 6
Latin America, 57
law enforcement, 18, 37, 38, 42, 44, 50, 57
laws, vii, 3, 4, 17, 18, 47, 62, 65, 77, 80, 81, 82, 85, 110, 111, 112
LEA, 18
lead, vii, 1, 99
legal protection, 42
legislation, 64, 70, 71, 83, 87, 100, 111
legislative authority, 112
legislative proposals, 101
lifetime, 53
light, 20, 39, 43, 46, 70
litigation, 68, 78, 80, 109
local government, 70, 84, 85
lying, 103

M

majority, 4, 23, 29
management, 86, 88, 91, 92, 94, 97, 98, 102
mass, 44
materials, 70, 106
matter, 75, 76, 86, 109, 112
media, 31, 38
medical, 38, 56
messages, 48
methodology, 32, 34, 35, 36, 44, 45, 53, 54, 59
metropolitan areas, 38
Mexico, 2, 3, 4, 9, 10, 13, 14, 22, 26, 27, 29, 30, 34, 35, 36, 38, 40, 42, 45, 46, 47, 49, 51, 53, 55, 56, 57, 58, 59, 61, 62, 63, 71, 82, 96, 99, 100, 101, 103, 105, 108
migrants, 2, 3, 4, 10, 27, 28, 29, 30, 31, 32, 34, 35, 36, 38, 40, 41, 43, 44, 45, 53, 54, 56, 57
migration, vii, 1, 2, 3, 4, 8, 13, 23, 27, 30, 31, 35, 36, 37, 38, 40, 41, 43, 44, 46, 47, 53, 58, 65, 73
Migratory Bird Treaty Act, 87, 92, 94, 97
military, 18, 22, 88, 89
minors, 43, 50
missions, 15
MMP, 27, 29
modifications, 62, 63, 70, 79, 104
mortality, 37, 38

N

NAGPRA, 95, 98
narcotics, 32, 44, 58, 104
National Ambient Air Quality Standards, 86
National Defense Authorization Act, 18
National Drug Control Strategy, 47
National Environmental Policy Act (NEPA), 80, 87, 88, 92, 94, 97
National Forest System, 91
National Park Service, 91, 98
national policy, 91
National Research Council, 11, 27, 50, 55
national security, 7, 52
national strategy, 30, 48
Native American Graves Protection and Repatriation Act, 95, 98
natural resources, 89
NCA, 92, 95, 98
negotiation, 106
NEPA, 80, 82, 87, 88, 92, 94, 97, 111, 113
New York, 47, 54, 56, 58, 103
North America, 59
NRC, 27, 53, 55

O

Obama Administration, 2, 3
Obama, President Barack, 18, 42, 47
obstacles, 84
obstruction, 95
offenders, 42, 49
Office of National Drug Control Policy, 5, 47

officials, 3, 11, 22, 30, 33, 46, 50, 55, 62, 64, 70, 71, 95, 101, 105
operations, 5, 7, 8, 18, 22, 42, 52, 56, 107
opportunities, 4, 22, 57
organ, 50
oversight, 21, 102
ownership, 22

P

Pacific, 19
pathways, 40
penalties, 1, 48, 87
Pentagon, 51
permit, 9, 49, 80, 81, 87, 90, 95
photographs, 25
plants, 88
police, 38
policy, 8, 9, 32, 39, 43, 44, 49, 83, 91, 94, 100, 102, 110, 112, 113
policymakers, 63, 74, 84
pollutant, 90
pollution, 86
population, 32, 35, 44, 45, 46, 54
port of entry, 10, 40, 58, 104, 105
potential benefits, 101
precedent, 110
preservation, 90, 91, 98
President, 3, 18, 42, 47, 89
prevention, 1, 5, 6, 25, 32, 38, 39, 46, 104
principles, 82
prisons, 50
probability, 7, 19, 27, 28, 34, 40, 45, 46, 55, 59
procurement, 94
project, 21, 68, 71, 80, 90, 101, 103, 104, 112
protection, 38, 43, 91, 92, 93, 94
public domain, 88, 89
public health, 90
public policy, 9
public safety, 33, 38

Q

quality of life, 2, 7, 33, 43, 70, 85

R

radar, 112
radio, 112
radius, 103
reasoning, 78, 111
recession, 36
recidivism, 2, 13, 14, 23, 25, 26, 31, 34, 35, 36, 43, 44, 45, 46, 50, 59
recidivism rate, 13, 14, 25, 26, 34, 36, 45, 46, 50
recreation, 97
recreational, 92
reform, 3, 44, 64
reform(s), 3, 4, 6, 19, 46, 47, 48, 49, 51, 58, 61, 63, 99, 104, 108, 109, 112, 113
regulations, 67, 81, 82, 87, 90, 92, 98, 110
regulatory agencies, 112
rehabilitation, 89
relevance, 110
religion, 95
requirement, 19, 61, 62, 64, 65, 68, 69, 70, 72, 73, 76, 80, 81, 83, 100, 104, 105, 106, 107
requirements, vii, 18, 62, 63, 64, 65, 66, 67, 68, 69, 70, 72, 74, 75, 76, 78, 79, 80, 81, 82, 83, 85, 87, 88, 89, 90, 91, 92, 93, 94, 95, 96, 97, 98, 99, 101, 103, 104, 106, 107, 108, 110, 111, 113
researchers, 31, 40, 46
resolution, 11
resources, 2, 4, 5, 6, 7, 10, 19, 22, 26, 31, 33, 34, 37, 38, 41, 42, 43, 44, 55, 63, 69, 71, 74, 75, 85, 89, 90, 91, 94, 113
response, 3, 5, 7, 21, 56, 74, 76, 100
restrictions, 3, 4
rights, 41, 43, 57, 91, 93
risk(s), 7, 22, 38
routes, 5, 40
rule of law, 41

rules, 86
RVS, 8, 21

S

safety, 33, 38, 85, 88, 103, 112
scaling, 101
schedule delays, 21
school, 41
science, 27, 40
scope, 71, 79, 80, 84
Secretary of Agriculture, 84
Secretary of Defense, 89
Secretary of Homeland Security, 19, 47, 54, 65, 66, 67, 68, 69, 70, 73, 74, 75, 76, 79, 80, 81, 82, 84, 85, 86, 102, 106, 108
security, vii, 1, 2, 3, 6, 7, 15, 17, 18, 26, 27, 30, 31, 32, 33, 34, 37, 42, 43, 44, 46, 47, 51, 52, 54, 55, 65, 69, 70, 71, 72, 76, 77, 80, 88, 99, 100, 105, 108, 111
Senate, 6, 48, 51, 52, 53, 54, 64, 70, 71, 76, 77, 100, 106, 107, 109
Senate Committee on the Judiciary, 52, 100, 109
sensor(s), 8, 19, 20, 21, 68, 69, 74, 76, 84, 85, 109
September 11, 6
shellfish, 94
shelter, 41
shortage, 42
showing, 79
Sierra Club, 81, 113
signals, 108
skeletal remains, 57
smuggling, 1, 5, 6, 8, 10, 18, 30, 49, 53, 63, 73, 107
Smuggling, 29, 30, 38, 58
solid waste, 92
species, 41, 87
specifications, 62, 100
stability, 94
staffing, 3, 5, 8, 17
state(s), vii, 2, 3, 7, 8, 18, 23, 30, 47, 53, 70, 75, 80, 81, 82, 86, 87, 91, 92, 102, 103, 107, 109
statistics, 50
statutes, 65, 67, 71, 77, 80, 81, 82, 103, 108
steel, 65
stock, vii, 3, 32
structure, 7
style, 8, 72, 110
Supreme Court, 67, 80, 82, 86, 102, 103, 110
surveillance, 1, 2, 5, 7, 8, 15, 18, 19, 20, 21, 22, 41, 43, 44, 68, 112

T

target, 7, 42, 109
Task Force, 13, 14
technologies, 5, 20, 21, 22, 52
technology, 1, 2, 5, 7, 8, 15, 19, 20, 21, 22, 52, 77
tension, 42
terminals, 6
terrorism, 32, 104
terrorist attack(s), vii, 1, 6
terrorists, 7, 19, 32, 46, 104
testing, 88
threats, 7, 33, 46
Title, 18, 51, 87, 88, 89, 92, 93, 94, 95, 96, 97, 98
tracks, 13
trafficking, 4, 5, 6, 18, 44, 107
training, 56, 88
transport, 89, 92
treaties, 101
treatment, 92
tribal lands, 58
tribal officials, 95
triggers, 65

U

uniform, 76
United Nations, 103
urban, 6
urban areas, 6
USA, 47, 51, 58

V

vegetation, 41
vehicles, 63, 72, 90, 103, 107
vessels, 22, 103
victims, 57
violence, 2, 37, 38, 40
violent crime, 38
visions, 42
vote, 71, 106

W

waiver, 75, 79, 80, 81, 82, 111, 112
Washington, 11, 46, 47, 48, 50, 51, 52, 53, 54, 55, 56, 57, 58, 59
waste, 92
water, 56, 86, 91, 92, 94, 101
water quality, 92
water supplies, 92
watershed, 97
waterways, 5
weapons, 7, 44
weapons of mass destruction, 44
web, 47
welfare, 90
well-being, 85
wetlands, 87
wilderness, 89, 91, 98
wildlife, 41, 43, 88, 90, 91, 92, 94, 97
withdrawal, 91
WMD, 44
workers, 3, 46
World War I, 3, 4, 101

Y

yield, 91